Crossing

Crossing

RECLAIMING THE LANDSCAPE OF OUR LIVES

Second Edition

MARK BARRETT OSB

MOREHOUSE PUBLISHING

An imprint of Church Publishing Incorporated
Harrisburg – New York

Morehouse Publishing, 4775 Linglestown Road, Harrisburg, PA 17112

Morehouse Publishing, 445 Fifth Avenue, New York, NY 10016

Morehouse Publishing is an imprint of Church Publishing Incorporated.

A record of this title is available from the Library of Congress.

ISBN-13: 978-0-8192-2290-9

Printed and bound in Great Britain

08 09 10 11 12   10 9 8 7 6 5 4 3 2 1

Contents

Preface to the second edition

'LISTEN,' says the black-habited figure on the TV screen. 'Can you *hear* it?'

There is a pause, and the camera pans across the attentive faces of five contemporary men.

'It's called ... *silence*'.

In my favourite moment from the recent BBC2 documentary series *The Monastery*, my confrere Father Luke Jolly offered that *Koan*-like introduction to one of the central practices of the monastic tradition. He was speaking to the five men who came to live among the monks of Worth Abbey for an extended Benedictine retreat in August 2004. Like contemporary *Everyman* figures, the TV retreatants set out to discover whether the Christian monastic tradition offered insights and values that could accompany them through life in the secular world. 'Can spending time in a Benedictine retreat really change your life?' as *The Times* asked in one of the multitude of follow-up newspaper articles spawned by the show. Through the experiences of those TV retreatants, could the practices of monastic life prove valuable to twenty-first century, post-Christian Britain?

The widespread response to *The Monastery* among the viewing public suggests that the answer is positive: *The Monastery Revisited* and *The Convent* were both screened subsequently. Perhaps something is changing in the spiritual climate of the contemporary world? Twenty years ago, what might have become an insightful TV feature about the monastic way as lived at Worth Abbey was transmitted not in colour, but in a strange sepia-like tone, as if to suggest an unbridgeable gulf between the arcane weirdness of monastic life and the here and now. It is difficult to offer much to the contemporary world if you live only in sepia. But *The Monastery* boldly went where only the *Mind, Body, Spirit* section in our high-street bookshops had gone before: into that territory where it is taken for granted that sacred traditions from the past can address the modern world and find that the audience is listening. The novelty is in taking classic Christian monasticism into a context where it is rubbing shoulders with holistic medicine, aromatherapy, yoga and New Age crystals. But when classic religious traditions climb over the wall of the ghetto to which we have sometimes confined ourselves, and sometimes been confined by others, we can become involved in encounters we would not have expected and be surprised by the outcomes.

I was a nervous first-time conference speaker at the University of Washington in Seattle in the month before *The Monastery* was filmed. *Information, Silence and Sanctuary* was an unusual event, bringing together academics, commercial managers, medics, IT specialists, craftsmen and monastics to consider the issues of information overload and pace of life in our technology-infused society: 'attention pulled in a thousand directions, and by the very technologies – cell phones and handhelds, email and the web, cable TV and satellite radio – that promise to inform and connect us', as the pre-conference publicity put it. All very true, I thought, but what might an English Benedictine monk have to say to Starbucks employees and Microsoft Corporation executives?

The conference organiser, Professor David Levi, had made the inspired decision himself to break down a few ghetto walls and to bring together secular students of the 'busy-ness' problematic with practitioners of ancient contemplative disciplines, and the dialogue he established quickly uncovered shared concerns where I had least expected to find them. Professionals from the worlds of medicine, education and business painted a picture of life in the modern city which, in terms of its impact on the human person, would not have come as news to the Desert Fathers in the third century.

The monastic tradition is alive with the awareness that, despite the frenetic activity in which the secular city involves us, many of us nevertheless experience an unfocussed sense of lack, a species of unreality. But *Information, Silence, Sanctuary* evoked precisely this analysis from the secular professionals, who addressed the conference not out of a religious conviction, but on the basis of their working experience. I listened to a doctor describe the response of many modern people to our sense of lack as a movement into what she termed 'hyperarousal'. When our activities and projects don't make us feel real, we – as it were – boost up the volume. As though more of the same thing that didn't work last time will make for a better reality-project if we simply replay it with the volume set much higher, we shout our life louder and louder, in the hope that next time we might be able to hear it.

In a state-of-the-art 21st century American conference room, I found myself describing the centuries old round of the Benedictine life to a passionately receptive audience of secular professionals. A monastery is a purposive environment, a sanctuary, in which every element of life is geared to aid *awareness*, what the Christian tradition terms 'recollection', for those who live within it. The use of space, of time, of sound and silence, movement, objects and attitudes, all contribute to the establishment of a unique context. In the scripted space of a monastery, a community of people can allow the layers of noise, physical and emotional, with which we surround ourselves first to be *noticed*, and then gradually to be peeled away or left behind, until the true Self can begin to emerge from the emotional thickets in which our preoccupied lives have hidden it. 'Can you hear it? It's called … *silence.*' In a monastery, the silence can become a place of sanctuary for the speech we call Spirit.

Monastic practices are not a panacea for the ills of modern

society, and it would be naïve to suggest that they can be. Neither my companions at *Information, Silence, Sanctuary* nor the retreatants in *The Monastery* would have allowed of this possibility for a moment. The point is rather that Christian monastic practices, like many of the disciplines of those religious traditions that have stood the test of the centuries, came into being at least in part as a response to the tidal currents of our hearts, set swirling by our busy lives, whichever century we live them in. These currents, often so difficult to address, frequently ignored or misunderstood, can become stealthy undertows, sweeping us to our destruction. The purposive environment of the monastery offers to those who care to engage with it one model of how the tides of the heart may find their harbour.

For the Christian, a monastery is more than this, of course. It is not true in any simple sense that a secular search for work-life balance is the same as what St Benedict calls 'truly seeking God'. But, to paraphrase the gospels, should I give my son a stone when he asks for a fish just because he asked for the wrong kind of fish? It was the rabbis of Israel who taught that when a man goes to synagogue it is a mistake to examine his motives for being there too closely. As is well known, we may begin a project for one reason but continue and finish it for motives that are very different. So the presence of the monk in an aisle of the modern spirituality-supermarket is an ambiguous sign. And how might it not be? We follow an incarnate Lord.

Those who read the first edition of *Crossing* have in many ways paralleled the response to Benedictine life among the audience of *The Monastery*; and I would like to thank here all those many people who made contact with me to tell me how the book has affected them. It is not always easy to address an audience when you cannot see their faces. Thank you, therefore, to everyone who has told me something of their own journey through the landscape I have sketched out here.

My concern when I wrote *Crossing* was to offer a way for those who do not live in monasteries to access something of what is a daily experience among us supposed religious specialists. I hoped that the reader would find that we monastics — so often the shadowy medieval figures of media-gothic — are in reality fellow-seekers, apprentices training among the tools of a spiritual workshop. I suppose you might say that I was trying to put some colour into those sepia tones I referred to earlier.

But two reactions to the book struck me particularly forcefully. The first was the impact of the patterning of *Crossing* after the shape of the monastic day, with its rhythmic pulse of worship; and the other was the extent to which my attempt to share a little of the journey of my heart, in Chapter 3, resonated with readers' own experiences. These two topics, I can fairly report, dominated my postbag. Readers commented on how they had, in many cases, returned to the practice of the Divine Office after an absence of a few years with a new excitement, or were embarking on it for the first time. They also remarked how moments in their own life's journey had features in common with what I describe as the movement 'into the labyrinth'. When I ask myself why these particular issues stand out, I return to my encounters at *Information, Silence, Sanctuary*.

I have referred to the monastery as a 'scripted space', in which all the elements of life are directed towards a specific end — recollection. Within this overarching shape, the pattern of the monastic day amounts to a purposive temporal environment built out of minutes and hours, coloured by the strong moments of the Divine Office. It is neither a shapeless grab-bag, loaded with random events, nor a featureless grey plateau, stretching from nowhere to anywhere. Whether this regular patterning of time is practiced in a monastery, or adapted in various ways to our lives in family or work contexts (for example by saying Morning and Evening Prayer daily) such a shaping of the day is a crucial tool in the process of learning to listen. When this patterning of time degenerates, we term it 'routine' and find it both oppressive and depersonalising. Perhaps it is for this reason that modern life has taught us to distrust it. But it seems that the further our society at large has moved away from a real appreciation of the beauty and power of the patterning of time, the more individuals and groups have found themselves drawn back to examples of lives regulated by a sense of temporal balance, structured around a framework of meaning. It seems to me that it is here that readers of *Crossing* unite with the other groups to whom I have made reference, appreciating the witness of the Benedictine tradition to the crucial role that temporal patterns can and do play in our lives.

It is from such temporal frameworks as the pattern of regular prayer provided by the Divine Office that monastics enter both the silence of recollection and the speech of community or activity; and in all of these events the practice of listening forms the uniform backcloth against which the variegated textures of all our other encounters can stand out. This is a listening of the heart and to the heart, what the secular world might call a 'reality check' – *am I really here?* As I suggest at several points in *Crossing*, this is perhaps one of the hardest questions to answer honestly, and – when it is answered – one of the hardest answers for us actually to hear. At times, the honest answer can be quite devastating; which is why I believe the individual seeker is in need of the community so as to be able either to ask or to begin answering the question that real listening poses. Here again, readers of this book have suggested to me that they have found support in monastic communities as they asked their own *reality check* questions.

Not long ago, my attention was held by a front page story in *The Times* headlined 'A nightingale's song can damage your health'. It seems that traffic noise in large cities is causing nightingales to sing so loudly that they end up making as much noise as a motorbike exhaust at full throttle. Technically, the newspaper correspondent points out, the unfortunate birds are breaking the law by exceeding legal noise levels. Like the nightingale, in its hyperaroused effort to out-sing the sound of modern life, each of us can opt to shout more and more loudly to ensure that we are properly heard. Alternatively, we can choose to listen.

'Can you hear it? It's called *silence*.'

Mark Barrett OSB
Pentecost Sunday, 2006

Introduction

'DON'T YOU GET *bored*, praying five times a day?' my students ask me.

'Yes,' I tell them. This always stops the conversation in its tracks, because it was not what I was supposed to say. Being a monk, I have realised, apparently makes me a special kind of person who does not get bored in prayer. *Ojala!* as they say in Spain – 'Would to God that it was so!'

In some situations, the young are an excellent reality check. But they can also be gloriously wrong. I have yet to meet a priest or religious who doesn't struggle with prayer, at least as much as any business executive or working mother. I remember a religious sister telling me that the first thing she learned as a novice was how to fall asleep on her knees.

That stylishly wicked author Muriel Spark in her novel *The Abbess of Crewe* (which is, among other unlikely things, a satire on the Watergate crisis set in an English Benedictine convent) imagines a Lady Abbess with a striking approach to the difficulties of a life of prayer.

While her sisters gather in choir to sing the psalms, the steely and silky Abbess Alexandra – from her high place 'too far from the choir for the nuns to hear her voice except when she sings a solo part' – chants in English not in Latin, so that 'her lips move with the others but discernibly at variance'.[1] She is, in fact, reciting the Romantic poets, having reached the conclusion that English poetry more adequately expresses the yearnings of her exalted soul than do the merely official liturgical texts.

Perhaps the Abbess gets bored too. She has noticed there is

[1]

supposed to be a relationship between the words of our prayers and the experiences of our lives. She has also perceived the dilemma that there is, all too frequently, a mismatch. But Spark's satire is surgically exact. Abbess Alexandra has not passed between the horns of this particular dilemma in arriving at her solution: she has simply lopped off one of the horns.

Boredom is one of the many inevitable obstacles we meet on the spiritual path. But when boredom is the *first* experience that religious observance calls to mind, something has gone wrong. This is a symptom of a gulf that can open up between the stuff of our lives and the practice of prayer, leaving us feeling that the spiritual life really is not for us. This gulf can be easiest to spot in public worship.

We must all have arrived in church for Sunday worship, at one time or another, preoccupied by a major event in national or international life, only to discover that at no point in the liturgy does the reality of this event or our concerns about it appear to be acknowledged. At Christmas, for example, we might sing 'O Little Town of Bethlehem' without even once adverting to the tragedy unfolding for the present inhabitants of that 'little town'. We never expect that a contemporary event should form the whole context of the community's worship, nor would we want it to. But we can be left puzzled, possibly offended, by the fact that the events we were concerned about seem (to judge from the service we have just celebrated) never to have happened at all. When the issue in our hearts is even closer to home – family tragedy or a personal anguish – the painful mismatch can be still more acute.

It is not only when issues that bother us are ignored that churchgoing can be alienating. I know many people who find it a source of deep dismay to discover that they themselves are 'invisible' when they go to church. Single people, the young who are no longer children (especially if they are women) along with many others, can form the view that the cycle of the year's liturgy is directed at someone other than them. Examples could be multiplied, and I have no doubt that most of us could supply our own moments when it dawned that – as far as the liturgy was concerned – we were not really there.

'Mind the gap', passengers on the London Underground are frequently reminded. Perhaps the same warning should sound out in all church porches. The language and symbolism of worship, the things we say and do in churches, can exclude rather than involve, just as they can mystify us rather than deeply engage us. At the same time, the fragmented and confusing demands we can face in our work, family and personal lives can be made to seem out of place in a religious context.

If this 'gap' is most obvious in public worship, it is most damaging and hardest to address when we meet it inside ourselves. It can often take the form of a gulf between our lives, awkwardly composed of rough edges as they are, and the practice of personal prayer, in which we may expect neatness and decorum to prevail. Instead of bringing our faith and our experience closer together, our prayer life consists of simply playing our spiritual 'hundred best tunes' over and over again, like certain classical radio stations, while our difficult lives go on a hundred miles away.

Many people today are looking for a new sense of depth in their lives, for some way of moving beyond the world of commercial surfaces that surrounds us. We sense, sometimes inchoately, that we are only touching the fringes of things – we are like children playing with pebbles, while an unexplored ocean waits before us. Many signs around us point in the same direction, so that while Britain apparently tires of churchgoing, a generalised 'spirituality' is booming: everything, from the New Age shop in the High Street to the Finding Values in the Workplace seminar at the office, repeats the same message. It is as if we are all looking for ways to inhabit our own lives more fully.

Consequently, as the twenty-first century dawns, the secular seeker and the religious believer have more in common than ever before. Although our approaches to the quest may differ, we are both seeking to be truly awake to the presence of the divine in the mundane. But we do not know how to do this alone. As members of a faith community, we will reasonably look to our

[3]

religious traditions and patterns of worship to help us through this process, and can face disillusionment if we discover that – far from leading us deeper into our experience – our religious observance simply sits at some distance from it. If the Abbess of Crewe represents one extreme solution to this dilemma, and that a poor one, what alternatives do we have?

The latin word for priest, 'pontifex', translates literally as 'bridge builder'. Faced with the perception that Christian prayer is either boring or irrelevant, and that it probably has little to do with the lives we lead, 'bridge building' is the task of the whole believing community, not simply of the priest. We need to make connections, to build bridges that will connect the disparate elements of our lived experience with the tradition of living faith we have received, and in doing so to allow sense to emerge.

This book is a small attempt to undertake just such a task of bridge building. I am neither a theologian nor an expert on Christian spirituality, but I have spent more than twenty years trying to make sense of my own life using the tools provided by the monastic tradition of the Roman Catholic church.

I began my life as a monk with the conviction that, if I threw myself into it with sufficient vigour, the tradition passed down through the centuries would, as if by magic, provide me with the answers I was seeking to all life's dilemmas. I vividly remember attending the fifteen-hundredth anniversary celebration of the world-wide Benedictine order in Westminster Cathedral and Abbey in my first year as a novice monk. It was heady stuff, but I was wrong to think that even fifteen hundred years of tradition carried any guarantee of right answers for the individual aspirant. I was wrong even to suppose that answers are what the tradition provides.

In the incarnation, God went native in creation. It took me a good few years to notice this fact and draw the inevitable con-clusion: faith takes us deeper into the reality of human living, not away from it. St Luke tells us that Jesus 'increased in wisdom and in stature, and in favour with God and man' (Luke 2:52), which was exactly what I had thought I could avoid doing. But there is no other route to holiness than the route provided by the simple practice of human living. And so I have tried to become a bridge builder, spending my time learning how to grow in faith by living, and how to grow more alive by fidelity and prayer.

If our faith statements are to speak to us of a God who becomes incarnate and of transcendence made immanent, then they must help us to understand the events that happen to us as the first place to look for God working in our world. Spiritual language must take us further into our own experience (especially when that experience may seem to be fragmented, negative or even hostile to concepts of God), not away from that experience.

An older form of catholic spirituality spoke of the cultivation of the garden of the soul. In many ways this is a delightful image, but it runs the risk of suggesting a set of approaches to spirituality which could be less than helpful. A garden is, of its essence, an area set apart and exclusive – there is much more outside it than inside. We control and regulate a garden, choosing carefully what grows. We may not always succeed, but this is the theory! Rather significantly, if theory and practice don't tie up, we will probably suppose that we have failed as gardeners. 'Garden' can suggest the neatness of a suburban lawn, the white picket fences of a small town. Inevitably, we will discover that much of our life-stuff consists of weeds, still more likely is the idea that much of what happens to us is outside the garden, and not appropriate material for cultivation. At the same time, 'soul' has itself become al-most the name of a something that we possess, a sort of spiritual organ – a little like the heart or the liver, but ethereal. It does not immediately suggest the sheer scale of life as we discover it: not a possession to be protected but a living and changing gift, to be accepted.

In place of the image of a garden – usually small, enclosed, neat and trim – I shall pursue the image of a landscape, in all its variety and glory. The landscape is a wide, wild place. It has beauty, but it also contains terror. There are paths through densely forested areas, and some high ground may be quite impassable. It is unpredictable, and the task that presents itself in a landscape is less the task of cultivation than of exploration, reclaiming the territory that should be ours.

The title of this book, *Crossing*, is borrowed from that of a painting by the contemporary artist Luke Elwes.[1] *Crossing* is an abstract landscape, at once the earth from space, a map of innumerable root-like pathways across a desert and a patterning of light and colour. The painting combines meandering lines, paths which unfold acrosss it's surface, with innumerable tiny crosses that mark the way - the very warp and woof of the brushwork. At the same time, the overall shape of the painting seems to lead us through a movement of light and dark that is both a single day and the pattern of a lifetime. This is a painting that invites us to become travellers in the landscape of our own lives. As the artist himself says:

> The lines are the paths of our own life, and the meandering course of all life, of branches, trees, roots and riverbeds. In their uninterrupted movement lies the search for markers, the signposts we need if we are to draw our own maps.[2]

From this painting arises the theme I shall be exploring in the chapters that follow: reclaiming aspects of the landscape of our life by exploring the markers offered in the shape of the monastic day. We shall be crossing the hours of the day, and in so doing crossing the landscape of our life. The signpost-like crosses within the painting suggest crossroads, marked out decision places where a series of possibilities exist. We shall see that each of these markers that punctuate the day stands at a point where we have significant choices to make about how we will understand ourselves and how we will find God at work in the lives we lead. The shape of the day will itself become an image for the pattern of our lives.

In the game of chess, bishops move diagonally. If we extend this fact into a metaphor for religious life, we might have – for example – the learned and agile Dominicans springing forward like knights, with that interesting little sashay to one side at the end of the move, while the Jesuits would move in straight lines, purposefully advancing across the board to achieve great things – the rooks of the religious life. By contrast, Benedictines, the monastic order to which I belong, would be hopeless chess pieces, because we tend to move in circles, a skill not much sought after in the game of chess.

Yet a circle is the shape most of us tread out in life: whether we live alone or are busy with the many tasks of family life, routine is the stuff we all work in. Days, months, years – the pattern repeats as regularly as the moving hands of a clock. Through the ages, monks have been characterised by the regularity of our way of life. The whole of the monastic life is founded upon patterns of repeated experience – the routine of daily prayer at set times, the times of work, of relaxation with the community. The recurrent cycle of the liturgical seasons as the year comes and goes is another, larger scale, version of the same pattern.

A monastery can seem a world apart from the lives most people lead. Recognising the circles we all tread out, though, can make of monastic spirituality, which could otherwise appear distant to those who do not live behind monastery walls, a spirituality relevant to anyone who has to cope with a pattern of repeated experiences.

The monk's day in any monastic community is structured by the liturgy of the hours: these are the times of community prayer that follow the circle of the day. Vigils is the pre-dawn office of readings and psalms. Lauds, the morning office, begins the working day. The Midday Prayer occurs at noon, and Vespers is sung as evening comes. The night office, Compline, takes us into the dark again. These moments constitute a framework for the spiritual life of monastics, a series of steps along the path by which we cross the hours of the day.

The chapters that follow use this pattern of crossings to provide a series of reflections on finding the presence of God in aspects of our regular experience, a process which I hope may assist the seeker in mapping the paths of his or her own life. Each chapter focuses on a specific moment in the liturgy of the hours, finding in each office a way into aspects of experience and Christian tradition which I hope are not uniquely monastic but more broadly human and so useful to a wide range of readers.

Rising in the morning for Vigils provides the starting point for a chapter which reflects upon the edges of the day, and so upon moments from the margins of experience. The markers here are the elements of life we frequently ignore or neglect, precisely because they have been pushed to the edges of our lives. Reluctance and fear of engagement are important here: will we even choose to begin the spiritual journey?

Lauds is the office of praise which begins the day, and in the act of praise – which calls us to step beyond ourselves – we can see a symbol of the step we must take if we are to move beyond the reluctance of the previous chapter. When we choose to undertake a task we engage our creative imagination to project ourselves forward into the future, and it is here, in the imagination, that we often hear the voice of God.

The middle of the day is the mid-point of the journey; this is the moment when confidence can fall away, the path can seem lost, and crisis can intervene. But there are many moments when it is difficult to tell the difference between being lost and being on the way. All travellers live with the possibility of losing the way. Here we will address the moment when our path must change, when we need to set out in a different direction.

The office of Vespers invites us to engage in a process of reflection on the journey as the day moves towards evening. This is the task of looking back, learning from what has already been, the process of 'chewing over' experience and reshaping it in order to learn lessons only available from a later perspective. Here we allow the landscape to reshape itself from novel vistas, and perhaps a sense of wholeness will emerge.

As darkness falls again, in the candlelight, the night office is chanted. This is the moment of letting go, and stepping into the dark. A daily reminder of the mystery of death that awaits us all, and a statement about the fact that all journeys have endings.

It might appear paradoxical in a Christian context to suggest so powerful a focus upon our own experiences. After all, do we not hear Jesus summoning us to self-forgetfulness: 'whoever hates his life in this world will keep it for everlasting life' (John 12:25). But the true paradox is that only those who already possess a clear sense of themselves can let go of this and move to the detached love of all to which we are indeed called. There is a world of difference between burying my half-formed sense of myself in the ground, like the unfaithful servant of the parable of the talents, and letting go of my self into the loving hands of God. In order to be self-forgetting we need to develop a clear, strong sense of ourselves, not avoid ever having one in the first place. We can only give away what we have; what we do not have in the first place cannot be surrendered.

As I began work on writing *Crossing*, I shared my plan for this book with a friend, who made suitably approving noises. I was preparing to think myself very clever when he pointed out that my analogy between the shape of the monk's day and the overarching pattern of the spiritual life had been used before. This did not completely surprise me, but I did wonder which father of the church, which great medieval mystic or counter-Reformation martyr it was with whom I was sharing an insight.

I was not expecting to be told about 'the Holy Lunching Friars of Voondoon' who sprang from the fecund imagination of Douglas Adams, author of *The Hitchhiker's Guide To The Galaxy*. According to Adams, the Friars 'claimed that just as lunch was at the centre of man's temporal day, and man's temporal day could be seen as an analogy for his spiritual life, so lunch should (a) be seen as the centre of man's spiritual life, and (b) be held in jolly nice restaurants.'[3]

Far be it from me to disagree.

REFERENCE
1. Further information about Luke Elwes and his work may be found at www.lukeelwes.com

1

The Piper at the Gates of Dawn

The Vigil Office

At least we know for certain that we are three old sinners,
That this journey is much too long, that we want our dinners,
And miss our wives, our books, our dogs,
But have only the vaguest idea why we are what we are.
To discover how to be human now
Is the reason we follow this star.

W. H. Auden, 'For The Time Being'[1]

IF THE RESURRECTION of the dead is anything like getting up in
the morning, I am not completely convinced that I want to be
included. There are few experiences I loathe with the intensity I
feel for that moment when the alarm clock calls me from beneath
the duvet. I stumble into the darkness of the still benighted world
fully convinced that sleep is better than prayer, as the *muezzin*
really should sing out.

For a few moments, for more than a few, it can seem that the
whole business of monastic life, this dedication to a life of prayer,
is actually a terrible mistake.

Monks are neither the only early risers in our society, nor the
earliest. But, along with early morning radio presenters, it may
be that we are among the most persistent. Every morning, in
every monastery, an early morning office of prayer and readings
calls the sleepers from their beds. I know that at least one rises
reluctantly.

Coffee helps, I find – at least with the early rising for the vigil office. To my dismay, I have not yet found an equivalent stimulant for the life of the spirit. At the back of my mind there still lurks the pious hope that it gets better with time. 'The first fifty years are the worst', a senior monk in my community used to say. This claim I have yet to confirm.

Stanley Spencer, an artist who in canvas after canvas explored the theme of resurrection, seems to have understood my dilemma. Many of his paintings present figures, clothed or naked, young and old, rising from the sleep of ages as if from a good night in bed. They are depicted in village graveyards in his native Cookham or elsewhere. There are those who yawn, those who spring into vigorous action, those who are still lounging languorously within their graves. But in several of Spencer's resurrection scenes we can sense that more than one of the figures stirring from his or her flowery grave does so with dismay. There is one remarkable canvas, to be found in London's Tate Modern, in which a small group of labourers with crowbars are to be seen, breaking open a series of graves as if to force the sleepers – in spite of themselves – to rise. I find the image haunting. Lazarus, hesitant, lingers on the threshold of the tomb, but other hands will propel him into the light.

It is reassuring to me as a monk that my less than enthusiastic approach to the business of prayer in the early morning is familiar not only to a contemporary artist, but also to St Benedict. The author of the *Rule for Monks* knows well that at least a proportion of the brethren in the communities for which he writes will sometimes succumb to what he terms the 'excuses of the sleepy'(RB22). Benedict envisages the more energetic early risers offering words of encouragement to their soporific confrères. He goes on to suggest that those who oversleep, arriving as late-comers to the early morning office should join their brethren in choir, not wait politely outside, because if they were to do this they might simply fall asleep again. Only too true. I suspect that there isn't a monk in the world who hasn't decided at least once that 'it's too late to get there', and curled up again for an extra half-hour's sleep. The author of the *Rule* is not simply concerned about community discipline when he makes these points: Benedict knows well that the darkness of the hour before dawn is a difficult moment for his monks.

It is the rawness of the vigil hour that makes me reluctant to face this beginning to the day. My pre-dawn self is defenceless, bleary-eyed. Half an hour focusing on psalms, biblical readings and patristic texts is not calculated to boost the ego. Instead, I am hard up against those aspects of myself that later in the day will be hidden beneath the polish of daily sophistication. Facing my own neediness, my boredom, my emptiness, or my preoccupation – that's the task of this first moment of the monastic day. Later, I shall be protected from having to face this exposure. The company of others, the demands and rewards of my job, the fact of a social position and the status that accompanies it, priesthood, or just my ability to clothe myself in the trappings of illusion, will disguise the nakedness of this first moment of the day. But for now, I am on my own, out on the margins of the day and exposed to the realities of myself. This is not an experience that most of us particularly wish to face. Benedict knows this very well, and consequently he provides support for those who – quite reasonably – find the going tough. I think that is all of us, at least once or twice a week.

There is nothing particularly heroic about this dimension of monastic life. I am very aware that many of the costly demands placed upon individuals in other circumstances are absent from my life – the midnight call of a hungry baby, for example, or the physical care of an elderly parent – but my point is not that there is some kind of heroic sacrifice involved in the early mornings of monastic life, but rather the reverse: the banality, the ordinariness of this daily waking moment. I am nobody special at this time in the morning.

Many dimensions of both our secular and religious cultures seek to cushion us from the harder edges of experience, and from the monotony of banal moments. A tape of monastic plainchant was sent to me recently: its title proclaimed it 'the ultimate winding down experience'. This is cotton-wool culture, the spiritual equivalent of recreational shopping in the mall. But the pre-dawn moment acts for me as a daily reminder that many aspects of life challenge the comforts I would so readily grasp. Here I'm alone, I don't want to do this, I'd rather not wake up. Perhaps I ought to find a way of dulling or simply avoiding this moment of the day?

It's not unusual to hear people speak of their favourite biblical stories: the emotionally moving, the edifying or the transformative in scriptural narrative. But, like the negative moments of the day, it's less common to address the theme of the stories we *don't* like. Personally, I have always had great difficulty with the story of the raising of Lazarus in St John's gospel, but — being deft at avoiding learning anything from my own desires or aversions — I had never asked myself why this should be. Eventually, and much against my better judgement, I had to use it as the basis for a period of reflection and prayer. I recognised that I found it almost unbearable to imagine the risen Lazarus stepping out of the tomb, and that my response to the call of Christ to do so was not joy but rather dismay.

Initially, my reaction surprised, even shocked me. As I reflected upon my reluctance to enter into this scene it became clear that it was closely linked to my feelings about the difficulty of the moment of waking and beginning again. One way to view the calling of Lazarus from the tomb is to consider *threshold* moments; those times when we find ourselves beyond the fields we know, and for that reason able to look back into our everyday from a new perspective. The vigil office, before we begin the new day, is such a threshold moment, and Lazarus' situation is surely one of the greatest examples. This man is standing on a threshold between two worlds: what does he see as he looks back?

A friend with whom I shared this question told me that in Cyprus Lazarus is identified as a local man, one of their own. And in Cyprus, I was told, they say that after he was raised from the dead, Lazarus never smiled again. A graphic illustration of the point.

There are moments when each of us stands outside the business of life, and looks back into the world we inhabit from a new perspective. We have moved out of our comfort zones, the places we know and are familiar with, and stepped into the 'non-places', as anthropologists call them, the impersonal in-between worlds of the airport, the rail terminal, or the network of motorways and their attendant service stations. These are spaces in which unmediated commerce reduces us to solitary individuality, where everything is fleeting, ephemeral. These places are no one's home, no one's territory. Rootless, we become ghosts, and like Lazarus we seem to have left everyone and everything we have loved behind. The solitary crowd surrounds us, we are alone with no status or story. Like the Cypriot Lazarus, we would be hard pressed to smile. But if we listen to what our heart is telling us, such moments can be a clarion call to 'wake up'.

I am glad that I found myself forced to examine my own dread of the 'Lazarus moment'. It has helped me to understand why I never want to get up in the morning. Because of the office of vigils, each day of the monk's life begins with such a moment; and so our attention is inevitably drawn to the moment when we must pass through the gates of dawn. This is an experience which, in other circumstances, might be disguised or cushioned. Vigils is difficult 'Because I do not hope to turn again', as Eliot puts it in his poem 'Ash Wednesday'.[2] Like Lazarus, we stand hesitating upon a threshold, but this happens time and again, day after day. My reluctance to rise joyfully to greet the call to vigils is a reminder to me of the fact there is something in me that really, truly, *does not hope*.

Nowhere is this more starkly presented than in the contrast between the beginning of the vigil office, the joyful invitatory antiphon 'Come, ring out our joy to the Lord; hail the God who saves us', which all recite together, and the struggle actually to arrive for the office. Benedict, conscious of the significance of this moment, instructs that this first psalm and response of the monastic day be recited 'slowly and deliberately'. He evidently wants to allow time for the latecomers to tumble into choir. But I sense that he knows well that in this moment the challenge of the Gospel impacts on the world of the monk in a very particular way, and therefore chooses to emphasise this moment. The Gospel is a constant challenge to *turn again*. But it is a challenge that always meets resistance, and that resistance isn't some superficial veneer, requiring only spit and polish to shift: it runs deep. *I do not want to ring out my joy to the Lord* every single morning before the sun has risen. This is a simple feature of the landscape of my life. The monastic way invites me, day by day, to notice this and to begin to ask what it signifies.

Everyone remembers the enthusiasm of the beginner – whether it is the beginner in the spiritual life or the beginner in a relationship. What is less frequently identified is the experience of someone who has been praying for some time, and finds that initial enthusiasm has waned. It is here that the sense of reluctance can be most powerful.

This reluctance to begin again is the first of what I want to call signposts in the landscape of life. These signposts often stand in places where I might not expect them, scattered across hollows and wooded places, hidden or overgrown, occasionally clear to see but frequently neglected. If I plunge on, ignoring the signs, assuming that I already know the way, I might simply walk in circles. But if I pause, attending to the signpost, what is there in these badlands of the soul that I should be noticing, and what can it tell me?

I have always been intrigued by a set of Japanese images, known together as the Ox Herding pictures.[3] The story of a farmer who loses and tracks his ox in the woods is told in a series of tiny woodcuts. Zen Buddhists find in these images a parable of the process of growth in the spiritual life. The relevance of the Ox Herding here is the profoundly simple point that before he begins to search, and certainly before he finds the ox, the farmer begins his whole journey by first *noticing* that the ox has disappeared. This is so obvious a first step that it is seductively easy to suppose that it can be dismissed and ignored. But perhaps it is exactly here that we should begin: *the ox has disappeared*.

For a reason I am not certain I understand, all our common sense instincts tell us to look towards what we have got, not towards what we lack. But Jesus appears to agree with the Japanese farmer of old, in pointing towards the ox who has gone. His parables tell of those who search for something they have lost or know they lack: shepherds set out to find stray sheep, widows seek out coins fallen to the earth, merchants pursue pearls. He who seeks, finds. The search begins from noticing a lack; an emptiness.

Implicit in any use of the metaphor of journey or search is the fact that we are not where we need to be. This is the first message we need to read from the signpost before us. What we begin to realise as we look closely at the landscape of reluctance is that we are some distance from where we need to be, and we don't know where that destination is. Although this discovery does not initially appear to be good news, it is important to allow its implications to sink in. We inhabit a culture that encourages us to see personal independence, our strengths as individuals fending for ourselves, finding our own way, as our primary virtues. Equally, we may well have learned to regard the recognition that sometimes we feel overwhelmed or lost, or need some kind of help, support or guidance as an admission of weakness or of personal failure. If this is so, then in the spiritual life as in secular life we will plunge straight ahead, imagining that we already know the way, or – at least – terrified to admit that we do not.

Monastic tradition says that this would be a terrible mistake. Only one who has travelled long and far in the company of others is able to travel alone, Benedict tells us (RB1). To set out alone and unaided is – inevitably – to go astray. Our first discovery must be that we don't know how to travel on from here, and that it is pointless to attempt the journey alone. 'It's better not to start from here', the countryman tells the traveller when asked for directions. In the spiritual life, this is our common experience: but we don't have the choice of an alternative starting point. We can only begin from here, and much as we may wish it otherwise, as we set out we realise that we are lost.

Paradoxical as it may seem, monasticism has always emphasised the need for travellers to begin the journey by realising that we are lost and do not know the way. In the *Rule for Monks* the first question asked about any newcomer to the monastic life is: does he or she truly seek God? Benedict lists a series of signs to look for in a true spiritual seeker, of which one is: Is he or she anxious for trials and humiliations? (RB 58)

This is not at first glance a quality that any of us would wish for – it appears, frankly, masochistic. Sadly, whole historical periods of monasticism have misunderstood Benedict along just those lines, producing a spiritual training which assumed that the rule for religious life was 'the bloodier the better'. But what the author of the *Rule* is actually pointing to is the experience I have called emptiness or lostness. This is a process of coming to face the reality about ourselves. Benedict is saying that seekers begin the journey by a frank admission that *alone we can do nothing.* To admit, even to ourselves, that we need help is to face real humiliation.

My first teacher in the monastic life used to say that he prayed that he might 'want to want' to pray. When I was a student for the priesthood, a wise theologian showed me that, in a very important sense, I do not want God. This is the only honest place from which to begin: we don't actually want to begin at all. We do not wish to engage in what Benedict calls the 'labour of obedience' (RB Prologue). The process of facing this reluctance is the task of conversion. It is not a matter of becoming, artificially, the enthusiast I am not; rather it is a matter of sitting with my reluctance, my resistance, and seeing it for what it is. Benedict calls this a *trial* or *humiliation*, and so it is – in the sense that it is a facing of the truth about ourselves. Honesty, above all honesty with ourselves, is the fundamental tool.

To encounter the God I begin to realise I do not know, I must be prepared to go beyond the contexts with which I am comfortable, and risk encountering the aspects of myself that make me uncomfortable. I must go into the desert. Biblical deserts are empty places – the context for the wanderings and temptations of Old Testament Israel, as well as the place of confrontation between Jesus and Satan. The desert is the land-scape of testing, but also of being lost. The desert is the threshold beyond the settled land. It was from a desert hilltop that Moses looked down into the promised land he knew he was never to enter. But, crucially, as the book of Deuteronomy reminds us, the desert is the place where Israel encounters the saving love of God:

> He found him in a desert land
> And in the howling waste of the wilderness
> He encircled him, he cared for him
> He kept him as the apple of his eye.
>
> (Deuteronomy 32)

In the monastic tradition, the desert is the place where monks go to confront the demons, and by facing the negative forces in themselves and their world to allow the light of the Gospel to shine in their lives. The Christian and Jewish traditions are replete with the significance of the empty place for our encounter with God.

There seems a world of difference between the harsh emptiness of the desert landscape and the tidy ranks of a Benedictine community gathered in choir for the early morning office. The vigil office may not look very much like 'the howling waste of the wilderness', even if it can sound that way on a bad day. But there is a direct tradition of life linking the activity of the contemporary monastic with the ancient struggles of the desert.

A story from the Desert Fathers, Egyptian monks of the fourth century, supplies the link. It was the custom for the newcomer to the monastery to ask a senior for a word to live by. Usually pithy and direct to the point of being almost gnomic, this word today might be somewhere between a rule of life and spiritual guidance. One such word left a certain determined newcomer dissatisfied. Anxious to live the life of the spirit to the full, he had been advised by an elder to sit in his cell, to pray at dawn and to pray at dusk. Feeling that there must be more to it than this, he sought better advice from a second elder. But this time he was told to pray only once, and otherwise to keep to his cell. Now thoroughly discontented, the young man sought out a third elder. 'Sit in your cell,' the old man told him, 'and your cell will teach you everything'.[4]

The young man clearly thinks he already knows the way; hence his search for someone who will tell him what he *wants* to hear rather than what he *needs* to hear. He has heard the call to conversion and wants to respond. He sets out on the way. The great thing that can go wrong at the point he has reached is that, having gone far enough to realise the beginning of the truth about himself, he snaps to attention (spiritually speaking), dusts himself down and sets about eliminating the problem. This is a sort of religious self-help, an attempt to lift oneself up by one's own bootstraps, and while it looks like repentance it is in fact the very opposite. Monastic tradition, which to the outsider can appear as the *locus classicus* of religious self-help, is actually about a process of facing the truth of our helplessness.

'If you see a young man ascending to heaven by his own will, pull him down again', said the Desert Fathers. To move forward wilfully is simply to dig ourselves further into the pit we have begun to identify. The traveller walks in circles, as the blind are leading the blind. The Desert Fathers knew that the first step on the path of repentance is to face the difficulty of actually being aware of one's lostness, accepting the reality of the emptiness within.

So the old man does not offer the newcomer a self-help manual. He wants him to sit down and notice the signposts in his own internal landscape. This is precisely the task that the monk is occupied with in the vigil office in any modern monastery.

There are two key points here. The first is the process of staying still and being attentive, learning to 'listen with the ear of the heart' (RB Prologue), as St Benedict expresses it. It is in the process of such an active listening that the monk comes to know the landscape of life, and begins to see God at work within that landscape. This listening may sound passive, but there is in fact nothing more active. Closely linked to it is the second point, which involves staying with a certain manner of life, accepting the need to keep working at the spiritual craft, which is a lifetime's project. Both of these points merit further exploration.

Vigils, unlike the other offices of the monastic day, contains a series of lengthy readings from scripture and from the fathers of the church. The primary task of the monk at prayer in the early morning is to learn to listen, in the first instance to sacred reading but further to that which the reading leads into and symbolises, namely, our own story, the landscapes of our lives. The *Rule* of St Benedict begins with a call for monks to 'Listen', to attend with the 'ear of the heart'. The essential monastic attitude, the author suggests is one which 'altogether shuns forgetfulness' (RB7). There could hardly be a clearer call to wake up. The *Rule* says, simply: please notice what is happening, attend to the landscape.

One who attends, who listens, is one who is truly present. Too much of my life is spent, like James Joyce's *Dubliners* character, Mr Duffy, at a short distance from my own body. The task of listening is that of learning to inhabit my own life, of returning to the place I need to be, because it is the only place I can *really* be. As W. H. Auden puts it in his poem 'In Transit':[5]

> Somewhere are places where we have really been,
>   dear spaces
> Of our deeds and faces, scenes we remember
> As unchanging because there we changed . . .

Auden suggests that if we are truly present, then there is a possibility that we may be changed. In Christian terms, this real presence to the moment we are living in is the prerequisite to conversion. But it can seem that what we encounter when we seek to be truly present can be profoundly discouraging – the trials and humiliations of which St Benedict writes. Perhaps two examples from outside the explicitly Christian tradition can assist us in recognising what is happening when we encounter the 'long wet tea time of the soul'.

Some years ago, I read about a practice called the Alexander Technique. I had always intended to find out more, and recently an opportunity presented itself. I had supposed the Alexander Technique to be a form of physical therapy, a training in posture and movement, but when I took the trouble to find out at first hand I discovered it to be much more.

F. M. Alexander was an Australian actor who began to encounter the debilitating problem of losing his voice on stage.

He was eventually able to overcome this difficulty by paying very close attention to the way he was carrying himself, how he was using his body, when the problem occurred. But the process of discovering this way forward gave birth to a series of insights into our ingrained habits – physical or otherwise – that have turned out to be valuable in many other contexts.

At the heart of Alexander's insights is the realisation of how little attention we pay to how we use our bodies. The careful hands of an Alexander teacher taught me to notice what I was doing with my body as I carried out such everyday actions as sitting and standing, walking or bending down. At first it disconcerted me to find that I didn't really know what I was doing as I sat down, or how I stood up, where I was holding my head in relation to my neck and my shoulders, or the nature of the walking motion. Together, we patiently explored processes of physical learning I had associated with childhood, and I discovered how little attention I had paid to what I was doing. And how, as a consequence, I was living at some distance from my body.

As I explored the teachings of F. M. Alexander further, I discovered how very difficult it is to be aware, let alone fully aware, of one's physical being on one's own. Although I read the books that were recommended, I became aware that it was only in the presence of the teacher – who taught through gentle touch more than by words – that I could begin to sense the real use I was making of my physical self. I became aware that the simple fact of having a body is very different from inhabiting it, from rejoicing in it. Only the teaching touch of another enabled me to find this out. There was a profound sense in which I experienced my body as a gift from another. My sense of my self is given to me by others, I realised. And this begins at the most fundamental physical level.

This was a very simple but profound lesson in waking up to the realities of the situation. I was astray, and didn't even know. Unless someone else had shown me, perhaps I would never have noticed at all. Before we can address the issues, we need to become aware of them, through a slow and detailed process of discovery. This is Benedict's trials and humiliations again, the process of being brought to face the reality about ourselves. Only in the place where we really are can we change.

My second example comes from the Buddhist tradition of awareness of breathing. Most spiritual traditions teach that stillness and silence are a crucial path to God, but it is Buddhism which has made the practice of a silent focus on one simple object of attention into a major spiritual art. Again and again I have found great insight in the unembarrassed stress of Buddhists on teaching a technique for meditation, and supporting the practice of meditation through group exercises, retreats and mentoring by experienced practitioners. This is a context in which we can encounter our own distractedness knowing that we are not alone in a foreign country.

To practise this form of prayer, the meditator allows her attention to focus on one experience only – the rise and fall of the breath. This is a listening of great simplicity but great power. Immediately I am aware of the chaotic turbulence of thoughts, ideas and feelings that are usually the background noise to the life of the mind. It can sometimes be that – for an instant – I am able to focus exclusively on one single in or out breath, but that immediately after this moment my mind has leapt away on a completely unrelated train of thought or remembered feeling. Then, like a patient owner training a new puppy, I bring my attention back to the breath. But, once again, I am conscious of the restless activity of that 'tree full of monkeys', the human mind.

Once more, I discover how little notion I had of what was happening – this time in my own mind. I need to be shown what is actually the case. Buddhist teachers stress the need to be very gentle and very patient with oneself at this point: a harsh self-criticism will undo any value to be found in the meditation, making spiritual progress unlikely if not impossible. I must accept, even rejoice in, the reality of my situation if I am to move forward, to change.

Prayer is a process of listening that is full of experiences I used to think I should not have. Anyone who prays will know the struggle to be present, to oneself and to God, the difficulties that accompany the attempt to live with that 'tree full of monkeys'. I believe that we sometimes talk too glibly of 'distractions in prayer', as if the experience was akin to driving down the road and catching a passing glimpse of something out of the corner of the eye. The reality, rather, is that at many times of prayer powerful emotional dimensions of myself will form the whole horizon of my attention: my anger with a friend, sexual fantasy, hopes or fears. Accepting and learning from what arises in me as I pray, involves a going where I have not chosen to go and is profoundly uncomfortable – even threatening. At this point it is crucial to remain with the prayer, but to be gentle. Judge not that ye be not judged, we are told. That is certainly true here. When I feel that I am failing, I want to blame someone – most probably myself, or blame the practice of prayer and give it up.

The medieval English author of *The Cloud of Unknowing* has this advice for the person who prays: 'A person is humble when he stands in the truth with a knowledge and appreciation for himself as he really is. And actually, anyone who saw and experienced himself as he really and truly is would have no difficulty in being humble'.[6]

Perhaps we are simply less courageous than the medievals, for the author of the *Cloud* supposes that seeing the 'degradation, misery and weakness of the human condition' is less problematic than being confronted with the 'transcendent goodness of God as he is in himself'.[7] I fear that we moderns find both experiences difficult, and certainly can be judgemental of ourselves in ways that are far from helpful when we begin to step into the darker regions of ourselves.

But can I stop blaming, and just notice what's happening? Unless we resist the temptation to judge ourselves at this point, we will disguise the landscape of our life, and hide from the challenge of stepping into the areas we find distressing, humiliating or uncomfortable. I do not blame valleys for not being mountains, I do not flee from lakes because they are not rivers. The landscape of my life deserves at least the same respect as the countryside I walk through. Let the landscape be, listen to the messages it brings. Perhaps what we encounter are some of the more difficult places in which to spend time, and the temptation to leave them is considerable, but it may be that they are the very places we need to notice. The Desert Fathers had a marvellous sense of how necessary it is to the spiritual life never to judge in a harsh and unforgiving manner. One story relates how a revered elder left a community that decided to condemn one of its number for a fault, saying 'I too am a sinner'; and a second story describes the response of a wise man to the problem of brethren who fall asleep during common prayer – 'If my brother falls asleep, I cradle his head in my lap'.

Several medieval English poems contain colourful depictions of the traditional seven mortal sins as personified figures, each speaking and acting according to the characteristic quality of that particular human passion.[8] Pride, for example, might become the strutting Lady Peacock Proud, while Avarice is depicted as a sallow figure, hungry and hollow, grasping out constantly towards all around him. In one text, Gluttony has established himself in an Inn, where more than a gallon of ale has been consumed and Sloth is 'all beslobbered, with gummy eyes'. These figures make a sorry procession of human weakness. Like a series of children's Mr Men characters, their speech and action reflect the character-istics of the vice they personify. But if we take them seriously as fellow human beings, rather than as a literary device, an important point emerges. The way each of these characters has chosen to act has changed his or her fundamental nature. The passions they entertain have altered their fundamental selves. In no way admirable, these unfortunates are trapped in a pattern of action which reinforces itself, until there is apparently nothing left of them other than the passion they personify.

I sometimes think that we may have substituted a sense of legal rules broken for a real sense of sin in Christianity. What comes from within, the frame of mind in which I exist, matters not because there is a rule somewhere that I am keeping or breaking. It matters because some ways of acting, springing from some states of mind, are fruitful and some are blind alleys in which we can become trapped. What we begin to discover in the listening process of prayer is the spiritual equivalent of what my Alexander teacher is pointing out to me about the 'use' I make of myself. Deeply uncomfortable as it is, we are encountering the realities of our minds and our hearts.

Dante's Hell has 'abandon hope' written over the gate.[9] This is a wonderful insight, because the abandonment of hope is the definition of hell. The sinners within find themselves caught in permanent and unchangeable states of sin *because* they have abandoned hope. The worst thing we can do at this point of realising the realities of our situation is simply give up and walk away – and this will always be an attractive temptation at these moments. This is reluctance, the abandonment of hope: *I do not want* to face the realities of my situation. Here we encounter the second aspect of 'sitting' – it involves a persevering resolve to stay with the path we have chosen and to see the matter through.

English Benedictine monks are trained in the tradition of Abbot John Chapman, a wise teacher of prayer, to 'pray as you can, not as you can't'.[10] This is good advice, but like most good advice it is capable of being misunderstood. One way to misunderstand Chapman's advice is to suppose that he is telling us to follow a way of praying until it becomes difficult ('I can't do this') and then try something else. I never cease to marvel at my apparently limitless capacity to see greener grass on the other side, whether in the spiritual life or in more secular or personal concerns. Nothing appears to interest me quite as much as the possible, nothing quite so little as the real. I have frequently misunderstood Chapman's injunction as an encouragement to try a little of this and a little of that. Only after some years did it dawn upon me that Chapman cannot have intended to produce a generation of spiritual dilettantes. Rather, he suggests that different paths suit different travellers: there is nothing to be gained by simply changing direction with great regularity, except possibly dizziness.

The daily round of prayer in the monastic office is an example of the spiritual perseverance that Benedict calls 'stability' and the Buddhists call 'taking the one seat'; that is, of dedicating oneself to a spiritual practice and staying with it. Benedict is strongly critical in his *Rule* of those monastics he refers to as 'gyrovagues'

(RB1): sixth-century equivalents of my desire to be off into another path. The gyrovague moves from monastery to monastery, the modern seeker from one spiritual practice to another, never staying anywhere long enough to learn the lesson that must be learned: only if we work at systematically following one path can the path take us anywhere.

A track worn into solid stone is a powerful image of such a commitment to working at the path. It takes many feet over many years to wear down a such a track: someone, many someones, had reason to tread this way, and reason to keep treading it.

Look carefully around the apse of an ancient English cathedral and the chances are that you will find a small doorway discretely but conveniently placed alongside the choir, from which such a stone stairway leads directly up to what used to be the common dormitory of a monastery.

It may surprise us today, but in pre-Reformation times several English cathedrals were the homes of Benedictine monastic communities: cathedral monasteries whose Abbot was the Bishop of the local Christian community as well as the father of his monks. For centuries monks worshipped in the choirs of these awe-inspiring buildings, living and working alongside the cathedral in monastic houses, which – if they are still standing at all – have today become museums, administrative areas, or facilities for tourists.

The stairway was the 'night stair' – specifically placed to speed the monk's journey from his bed to the night office of vigils. Like the fireman's pole, the night stair was the quickest way from the dormitory above to the church below.

The deeply worn slab-like steps tell a story: the very stones witness to the pursuit of the faith journey. These monks of old were people who not only set out, but who kept on walking. In their fidelity they point up in a powerful fashion the paradoxical quality of commitment.

Wearing a path into the very stones of the floor involves a profound dedication that overcomes discouragement and disaster, the monotony of the ordinary and the boredom involved in repetition. This is a task that we can appropriately call work.

Benedict is uncompromisingly aware that the spiritual life is a labour, a work, and that the monastery is a workshop. Images of the 'tools' required for the spiritual craft, of the monk as workman not only in the fields or in the kitchen, but in the life of prayer, abound in the seventy-three brief chapters of the *Rule*. This is the reverse of the perspective we frequently wish to adopt towards spirituality, which is not uncommonly presented today as a recreational pursuit: meditation for stress management, for example. There's nothing wrong with praying while you smoke, one monk is rumoured to have said, but a lot wrong with smoking while you pray. For Benedict, prayer is work, and the monastic office is the Opus Dei – the Work of God. The ability to remain faithfully dedicated to this task is the quality which Benedict sees as defining the monastic life, and – by extension – the whole enterprise of Christian prayer.

I have called this chapter 'The Piper at the Gates of Dawn', partly because in my own life the chanting of the vigil office so often acts as the harbinger of dawn, and partly because the experience of facing the reality about ourselves is the herald of a dawning light in the lives of those who patiently explore what it has to teach them. But I have deliberately borrowed the image of the Piper from Kenneth Grahame's children's classic, *The Wind in the Willows*. Grahame's charming story of the river bank and its variously generous, self-serving or eccentric inhabitants may not immediately appear to merit a place on a shelf of spiritual classics, but there is a parable waiting to be uncovered in the chapter whose title I have appropriated.

In Grahame's tale, his river-bank characters, Rat and Mole, like so many of the individuals I have been concerned with in this chapter, discover that something is missing. In the case of Rat and Mole, some*thing* is in fact some*one*: Little Portly, the baby otter, is missing. Portly is a regular adventurer and often disappears. But this time it is more serious.

The two friends, dismayed at their loss, cannot sleep. 'I simply can't do *nothing*, although it seems there's nothing to be done. We'll get the boat out and paddle upstream. And then we will search as well as we can.'[11] Although it appears hopeless, searching

[28]

is better than doing nothing: so, long before the dawn they set out upstream and into the wild wood.

As the moon falls away towards the dawn they explore the landscape of the benighted river bank, deserted and made unfamiliar by darkness. Grahame establishes in detail the newly strange features of their world: sounds unknown to them, shadows appearing as solid objects, the river itself now invested 'with a difference that was tremendous'.[12] This is the experience of standing outside the familiar details of life which I have called the threshold moment. On a dark night, when all is at rest around them, Rat and Mole set out into a landscape they seem never to have explored before. Although frightened and hesitant they press on, attentive to their search.

As they search, they are occasionally aware of a strange, beautiful and new piping music, never heard before. Caught and then lost on the breezes of the night, the music affects them deeply, drawing them on, until, in a garden-like landscape, they encounter the Piper himself, an awesome figure of holiness and transcendent power, the Friend and Helper, in whose care they discover their lost neighbour.

This moment of discovery has an ambiguity about it. There is joy in finding their friend, and the compelling attractiveness of the Piper himself. The companions know that the only appropriate response to the one they have met is worship; and yet this is not an easy place for them to be:

> 'Are you afraid?' the Mole found breath to whisper.
> 'Afraid?' murmured the Rat, 'Afraid! Of – Him? O, never, never! And yet – and yet – O, I am afraid.'[13]

If we can honestly face both these reactions as we set out on our journey, we may find the courage to press on. We may not wear a path into the stone, but, in this threshold moment before the dawn, we may 'discover how to be human now'.

2

The Vision of the Way

Lauds (Morning Prayer)

The girl dressed only in her falling grace,
From perfect shoulders to as perfect feet,
Lacks nothing, and her beauty seems to call
With one design in every track and trace.

Image of God, for so she is! He chose
So to portray desire of union
With the invisible, to which all tends.
The spirit clothed in flesh cannot disclose
Itself whatever other will is done,
Except in what it wears for human ends
                    C. H. Sisson, 'For Thomas à Kempis'[1]

CHOICES ARE DIFFICULT. There are always places where the road divides, and we have to choose one path or another. These crossroads are challenging places, whether the crossing involves starting a new job, beginning a relationship, or trying a religious vocation. Wherever our journey might take us, I am convinced that we are *summoned* to begin: we do not simply look around, decide and then walk forward unaided. Something about the path must first catch our eye. More often than not, we act without anything like full knowledge of what we will be letting ourselves in for. Looking back, we sometimes feel that if we had known, we might never have begun at all. What is it we see to encourage us into making such a remarkable leap?

The Desert Elders of Egypt told the story of how one monk, Lot, visited another, Joseph, to seek his guidance at a crossroads in his own life. 'So far as I am able,' Lot explained, 'I keep my rule of life, my rule of fasting, my prayer, meditation and contemplative silence; and so far as I am able I strive to cleanse my heart from wicked thoughts: now, what more should I do?' Joseph rose up in reply, and stretched out his hands to heaven, and his fingers became like ten lamps of fire. He said: 'Why not be totally changed into fire?'

This is an astonishing image. We catch a vision of fiery love as challenging to our usually rather prosaic modes of living as Jesus' statement to Nicodemus that he must be born again, or the instruction to the rich young man to sell everything and set out on the path of discipleship. The beginning of the transfiguration that we term faith is an ability to see beyond what we had supposed we understood. Somehow, it seems, we have to learn to look at our lives in a totally different light.

The first moment in our process of awakening, we have already discovered, is the difficult realisation of emptiness, of reluctance. In the delightfully earthy language of the Ox Herding images: the ox is missing. From such an honest openness follows the image that comes next in the Ox Herding sequence: the farmer sees traces of the ox's path. Here an event we could not have foreseen transforms our landscape from the night-shrouded terrain of reluctance into a bright pasture of engagement.

Lauds, the morning office of praise as the sun rises, is the moment when we glimpse the possibility of engagement. Something catches fire in our hearts, giving us the light we need to make a choice, to move forward. In the act of praise, we step beyond our small selves, and glimpse the greater Self. The landscape is suddenly flooded with light: gone are the fogs and badlands of reluctance. As the bright sun dawns across the landscape of our lives, we respond – as St Benedict puts it – by running with expanding hearts towards the manifestation of the divine that is dawning upon us (RB Prologue). Here is the signpost that signifies commitment.

Our daybreak moments – the events that teach us how to see

in a new way – can come in various fashions, like the sunrise itself. There are those for whom the rising sun of salvation dawns brightly in a single event, an event whose light floods their lives and never dims. But not all of us will be like St Paul, dazzled once and forever by the light of heaven. Perhaps more common is the gradual accumulation of many, sometimes foggy, dawns. We experience an incremental increase in the light by which we see, until we are finally able to discern the way ahead. However the light dawns for us, when we succeed in choosing the way and setting out down the path, it will be this dawn of vision that carries us forward.

One of the greatest crossroads one can approach in life is that of entering a religious tradition from outside. All of us who are members of a faith tradition must find ways of making it our own, even if we were born into it. But entering a tradition from somewhere else can be a daunting step. So, it was with some trepidation that at the age of seventeen I knocked on the door of a large town centre presbytery, hoping to find a priest. I intended to say to him, 'I want to become a Catholic'.

Like many unchurched teenagers before me, I was exploring the 'big questions' of life. I had begun to pray, I had tried out various forms of Christian gathering, I had even debated the pros and cons of the Catholic faith with a well-informed teacher. All of these played their part in bringing me to that presbytery threshold. Once I got through the door, I found warmth and humour. The Parish Priest offered wisdom, friendship and support. But it was not an anticipation of these qualities that got me over the threshold in the first place. The event that compelled me was a chance encounter with a beautiful girl on a student drama course.

A schoolgirl from a southern convent, she was the first person I ever met who identified herself as a Catholic. Chic and sophisticated, she had the Renaissance beauty of a Botticelli Madonna and – I remember – wore a small jewelled crucifix around her neck. Among a group of sincere but slightly dowdy would-be thespians this bird of paradise shone out brightly. My seventeen-year-old imagination was completely captivated. Something in me caught fire in the vision of charm and beauty this young lady represented.

I knew very little of the Catholic faith at this time. It glowed like an exotic mystery on the horizon of my mind. But this distant mystery, this sun that was almost rising, dawned for me in this beautiful girl and shone in the jewelled crucifix she wore. I didn't know it as I crossed that presbytery threshold, but she had kindled a flame that would guide me in a direction neither of us could ever have predicted. Forever after, the church to which she belonged, and which I joined shortly after meeting her, has represented for me an entrance into the vision of beauty that we call God.

Such significant moments have dawned for all of us. They are the 'soft places' of our life's landscape, in which it seems that eternity presses close upon time. Something, a person, a place, a work of art, evokes from within us – or is it from *beyond* us? – a vision that has the power to transform us. All at once we see into the landscape of inspiration, as our imagination takes winged flight, and – if only for a moment – all things seem to become possible to us. The reluctance that weighted our feet, the fear of the unknown or the laziness that can hold us back are all swept aside. The light has dawned – we cross the threshold, make the leap into the day.

This sense of wonder is at the heart of the principal morning office of the monastic day, Lauds or Morning Prayer. Every morning monks greet the rising sun of salvation with the gospel words of exultant praise: 'Blessed be the Lord, for he has visited his people, saved us and set us free' (Luke 1) – and it is from the act of praise that the office takes its very name. To 'laud' is to 'praise'.

Lauds is the celebration of God's new action which we have caught sight of in our everyday world. 'In the tender compassion of our God, the dawn from on high shall break upon us,' we sing in the words of Zechariah, 'to shine on those who live in darkness and the shadow of death, and to guide our feet on the road of peace.' In the light of this dawn, we reflect on the moments when we recognise the presence of God momentarily unveiled within the world. We give praise for the ending of the night, and are carried together over the threshold of the day by the declaration in the office of God's providential purpose.

There is something very special about the moment when the members of a Benedictine house gather for Morning Prayer. My community is privileged to live in a most beautiful part of Sussex (monastic communities tend to have an eye for prime sites!), and watching the dawn break over the woods and fields of the valley below the monastery never ceases to delight me: the world of nature is transformed. The community gathers once again in the choir, this time a gathering in the light, and our presence is a supportive gift to one another, a statement about our mutual commitment: the human world takes on new features. And the office of Lauds itself, a liturgy of praise full of psalms of joy and triumph, is a moment of ecstasy: we are called to step beyond ourselves. All of these powerful symbols state that God enters our world, as light, as brother, and empowers us to travel forward, as we respond to his call.

The Lauds canticle is Zechariah's *Benedictus* (named from the Latin of its first word, Blessed be the Lord). Surely, this song has found its place in this office because its image of Christ himself as the rising sun so appropriately links the dawn of day with the dawn of salvation. It is no accident that an image from the natural world is used to symbolise the presence of God incarnate. Our celebration of God's unfolding purpose coincides with the world's own physical unfolding in the glory of the dawn. The ending of the night profoundly alters the nature of the landscape we in-habit – both literally and figuratively. As the country around us, previously shrouded in the secrecy of darkness, is unveiled, the way before us becomes clear and we are set free to move forward with confidence. In the daybreak moment that transfigures the landscape we are granted a vision of the way.

Biblical books from Genesis to the Apocalypse explore the symbolic potential of light and darkness: 'Let there be light' stands at the beginning of a story that ends only when we are told of a city where 'night shall be no more . . . for the Lord God shall be their light'. The liturgy for Easter night picks up this pattern of thought, as the community enters the darkened church led by the 'Light of Christ' in the Pascal candle. In our faith statements, God opens the eyes of the blind, dawns upon those who live in darkness, and burns as a pillar of fire in the night. The physical seeing that light makes possible is regularly employed as a metaphor for our understanding of the ways of God. But in biblical tradition, seeing is more than just a metaphor.

Seeing a marvel, and finding the presence of God in what we see, is a frequent reality for the biblical writers. Moses is caught up into his role within the divine plan when he turns aside from his path, 'to see this great sight, why the bush is not burned'; the prophets are frequently asked by God, 'Look, what do you see?' and in the signs presented to them by the world of nature or the world of human action they recognise the 'dawn from on high'. Like the disciples who meet the risen Christ on the Emmaus road, their eyes are opened, their hearts burn within them and they recognise the one who was with them all along.

Each of these stories is an example of a specific, concrete happening. Unfortunately, we often speak of the action of God in much more general terms. Religious language should be vivid and direct, but more often it can appear abstruse and technical – worst of all, it can descend into a series of stale abstractions. But we do not meet God in the abstract. A beautiful girl, as the poet C. H. Sisson reminds us, 'may still attune/ Our instant eyes to catch the marvellous/ Which is not anybody's greedy prize'.[2] When we allow ourselves to 'catch the marvellous' – or, more often, to be caught by the marvellous – as it shines through the prism of our everyday encounters, we engage with the God who said, 'Let there be light'.

Wilson van Dusen, an American spiritual writer, describes a meeting with an elderly woman who was clearly close to death. She was anxious to hear from him that a glowing golden sun she had seen in a dream was a manifestation of God. 'I first thought of my standard reply, "We need to go into the dream and see what is in it". But then I was struck by the emotional impact of the larger situation. This old woman is dying, and it matters very much to her if she met God even once in this life. I said, "Yes, it was God," and we both broke into tears. But how sad. She had the marks of a very spiritual person, whose life was embedded in God. And yet she asks desperately if once she met Him. To me she represents most of mankind. She is already on her way, but she does not recognise the signs.'[3]

Van Dusen's old lady could be any of us. Our tragedy is that we have almost lost the ability to recognise the signs. We know the dawn when we see it, but it does not occur to us to see more than a ball of fiery gas. William Blake, the eighteenth-century English poet and artist, looked at the rising sun and saw a host of angels crying 'Glory to God'. But ours is an age of surfaces, we engage only with the immediate: the tedious litany runs from fast food to the soundbite. Ours is an 'instant eye', while the great art of seeing the signs is one that requires us to dip below the surface, something our education in empiricism teaches us not to do. This slower way of seeing takes a time we only grudgingly give, and an openness we are schooled by the suspicions of our time to consider gullibility. But if we can allow ourselves to unlearn some of our contemporary habits, there is a tradition of symbolic awareness that can assist us in finding the path we are looking for.

As soon as we attempt to engage with something beyond the surface appearance of things, we realise that we will have to acknowledge that we ourselves are more than the surface we present each day to the people around us. There is more to each of us than the 'I' of which we are consciously aware, and it is when we allow ourselves to notice the signs of God's presence in our world that this fact dawns upon us. The greater Self is an unexplored landscape, a territory with a vast, fascinating hinterland. We stand in a small area of light: there is much more out there of which we are unaware. Most of us are uncomfortable with the discovery that we have a lot to learn about ourselves, and the fear of the unknown that has always led us to huddle about the campfires of our culture will often send us back to the small circle of light we call 'our self'.

Modern culture is not very open to the symbolic interpretation of experience. Perhaps the mood is shifting, but for the most part our society remains deeply sunk in what Blake described as 'single vision and Newton's sleep'.[4] Blake considered the arrival of what we would now call the age of science as a profound limitation upon our ability to use symbolic imagination to understand the depths of experience. The mechanistic account of the universe that has been immensely productive in terms of scientific discovery has been a limiting factor on our ability to see the symbolic significance of our world — as Blake puts it, we only have 'single vision'. We see the surface, but we do not know how to understand the depths. We grasp the facts, but miss the meanings.

Often, we moderns need to be *taught* how to understand our experiences symbolically — we are symbolically dyslexic, needing a sort of remedial teaching, which would not have been required by people of an earlier age. It is particularly ironic that Christians, whose liturgies abound in symbolic moments, so often fail to respond to the signs that are staring us in the face.

My own sense of the symbolic has been profoundly affected by reading the work of the thirteenth-century Italian poet, Dante Alighieri. It was from Dante's great work *The Divine Comedy* that I learned a way of understanding the events of my own life symbolically, a way of reflecting on events and connecting meanings that modern culture had certainly not provided me with. The more I learned from Dante, the clearer it became to me that his sense of how to discern the presence of the divine in the mundane is something that is at the heart of the Benedictine understanding of life.

St Benedict takes it for granted that we can see Christ in the Abbot, in guests, in the sick brother, that we can understand why all the goods of the monastery should be treated as the vessels of the altar. But we read him as saying that we should treat these people and objects with respect. To respect and reverence is good, but this is not in fact what Benedict calls for. Like the old woman in van Dusen's story, he is looking at symbols — but unlike her, he knows how to read them.

If we consider Dante's attitude to a young woman who transformed his life, perhaps we will be closer to Benedict's real meaning.

When the poet was a boy of nine, he met the eight-year-old Beatrice Portinari quite by chance at a May Day party in her father's house. This was a meeting the world has never been allowed to forget. Such was Beatrice's impact upon the young Dante that when he came to write *The Divine Comedy*, his epic of hell, purgatory and heaven, the figure of Beatrice is at its centre as the poet's heavenly patroness.

Beatrice died tragically young, but while she lived the young Dante sought out every opportunity to meet her, or simply to be in places where he could gaze at her. 'Childhood sweethearts', we would probably think, and we would be right to do so. But if our understanding stopped there, on the surface, we would be missing the whole point. Dante tells us that Beatrice had become for him a revelation of the divine in bodily form. He sought her out because the beauty he saw in her made her the image of God for him. For Dante, she was a real presence of the glory of God – a personal sacrament of God's presence, in fact – and so he finds in Beatrice an image of other God-bearing figures: the Mother of God, the seven sacraments of the church, or the life of grace. Ultimately, for Dante, the presence of Beatrice is identified with the presence of Christ himself.

This is a step we would perhaps feel uncomfortable taking, but for Dante it was completely appropriate. Dante chose to portray his desire for union with the divine through the figure of Beatrice. But there is an important sense in which, for him, this was not a choice. For Dante, Beatrice was a vehicle of God's presence. The moment of revelation in which he was caught by the marvellous had never left him. When he looks at this 'image of God' he is guided towards the life of grace and ushered closer to the heavenly presence of God. She exalts his soul, she inspires a new way of life, a conversion in him.

Dorothy L. Sayers, who translated and commented on Dante's poem, makes the point well: 'Beatrice thus represents for every man that person – or more generally the experience of the Not-self – which, by arousing his adoring love, has become for him the God-bearing image, the revelation of the presence of God'. [5]

When I first encountered Dante's way of seeing the figure of

Beatrice I was given a completely new way of understanding the relationship of the sensuous and the spiritual. Our culture tends to present these two crucial and life-giving dimensions of life as polar opposites. In the figure of Beatrice, the two are united, and each speaks the language of the other.

'All is concealed, indeed, unless it speaks/ The language of the flesh and speaks in love', [6] writes C. H. Sisson. He urges that 'flesh understands, or spirit cannot teach'. This is a message that can be very hard to hear, because we are so poorly attuned to 'catch the marvellous' in the physical world around us. We are more comfortable with a strong division between the flesh and the spirit, especially if this dichotomy is presented in terms of the erotic and the spiritual. We can feel quite unsure how to address any attempt to identify the two.

A case in point is the approach we take to a biblical text like the Song of Songs, an Old Testament book so frank in its treatment of eroticism that it very nearly 'fell out' of the official canon of the Bible, and can still cause difficulty to some listeners when it turns up in the regular public liturgy.

Traditional biblical exegesis finds in this beautiful book a series of allegorical images of the call of Christ to the Church, and identifies the language drawn from the natural world or from human love-making as a set of symbols for the graces and gifts of the Holy Spirit. Most contemporary exegetes see the book as a collection of ancient near eastern love lyrics, having to do with a very erotic relationship between the poet and his bride.

But what is particularly fascinating is the fact that the mindset into which we have all been enculturated finds it extraordinarily difficult to connect these two ways of reading. It seems that for us moderns the Song of Songs must be either one thing, an allegory, or the other, an erotic love lyric – it is not allowed to be both.

In the Song of Songs the voice of the beloved is a summons to erotic love, without a doubt. But it is not only this. The Song is preoccupied with physical beauty, and with the impact of the beloved's beauty as a transforming power in the lives of the lovers. Further, by choosing to include this collection of poems in the sacred canon, the scribes of old were telling us something about themselves and their outlook. The culture that saw no contradiction between Leviticus and the Song conceived of our response to the physical world, to beauty and to the erotic rather differently from the way we have tended to see them. It seems that, like St Paul, they believed that realities in the physical world, especially when we find them attractive, had something to say about the relationship between God and the world of humanity.

The recent Hollywood film 'American Beauty' is a secular morality fable dramatising some of these issues. Its central figure is a middle-aged suburban professional, Lester Burnham. Lester develops an overwhelming infatuation for Angela, a friend of his teenage daughter. Lester is a truly contemporary figure – he can only respond to Angela's beauty as surface glamour. Although it seems that his vision of 'American Beauty' is rejuvenating and fulfilling him, it actually leads to his death. He is a man of the surface, trapped in a 'single vision' of the world.

By contrast, Ricky Fitts, a teenage outsider figure, is able to perceive what no other character in the film can see – that there is something more to the world around him than surfaces. He discovers beauty in the most unlikely places. Ricky describes his feelings as he watches a wrinkled white plastic bag, floating in the wind: ' . . . this bag was just . . . dancing with me. Like a little kid, begging me to play with it. For fifteen minutes. That's the day I realised that there was this entire life behind things, and this incredibly benevolent force that wanted me to know there was no reason to be afraid. Ever.' It is Ricky who – uniquely in the film – can sense transcendence: 'Sometimes there's so much beauty in the world I feel like I can't take it . . . and my heart is going to cave in.'[7]

The world portrayed in 'American Beauty' is disturbingly familiar. The connections between our surfaces and our depths have become very tenuous, when they can still be found at all. In this film, the individuals who appear to be successful are trapped in a world of sterile surfaces, unable to connect with any sense of meaning outside themselves. Only someone who is apparently a misfit senses that there are dimensions beyond the obvious.

For our society, the creation and perception of beauty are in danger of become the exclusive province of experts. Instead of being a feature of our lives, a way we choose to look beneath the surface of the people and the contexts in which we live, we have put beauty into galleries or confined it to the discussions of aesthetes. We cannot see the beauty of the middle years and of old age, because we have confined beauty to the professional glamour of the catwalk. It is something that now exists on the fringes of our lives, not something we find all around us. The native American Navaho tribe prayed:

> With beauty may I walk
> With beauty before me may I walk
> With beauty behind me may I walk
> With beauty above me may I walk
> With beauty all around me may I walk.[8]

To our ears this can sound either self-indulgent or precious – which tells us a lot about how we have devalued the notion of beauty. Surely, the Navaho people who originated this prayer were asking that they might be open to see the depths that were waiting all around them, able both to look at and to look through their immediate surroundings, to find the world of revelation coming to meet them.

According to the Gnostic Gospel of Thomas, Jesus said: 'Know what is in front of your face, and what is hidden from you will be disclosed to you. Split a piece of wood; I am there. Lift up the stone, and you will find me there'.[9]

Perhaps we need to recapture something which these older cultures appear to have taken for granted: a sense of reverence, which can even become transcendent wonder, before simple details of the mundane, a wonder that is experienced in all dimensions of our humanity. This may be astonishment before beauty, whether that beauty is the glory of the natural world, the physical beauty of a lover, or the aesthetic appeal of a work of art; it may be wonder at the fidelity of a couple, the wisdom of an elder, the energy of a colleague. Whatever the object of our gaze, the reason for our sense of wonder is the recognition that what we are seeing is an aspect of the presence of God.

When our sense of the symbolic is awake, we can be constantly surprised by moments of light. Whether it is Dante's response to the figure of Beatrice, the lovers in the Song of Songs, or my own more personal encounter with a lovely girl on a drama course: there is no exclusivity, no 'single vision' as Blake would have termed it. It is perfectly possible for a physical, historical human being, in all his or her glorious uniqueness to be just who they are, and at the same time to be the vehicle of the divine presence to us.

Benedictine life is full of reminders that each monk is a sacrament of the presence of God to his brethren. The times of community prayer, for example, are a daily affirmation of the commitment of the community's members one to another. Sheer physical presence – something that abbots always have to nag monks about – matters immensely. I remember being very struck as a novice by hearing of an abbot who told his community: 'Fathers, please do try to fit the office into your timetables.' The comment might surprise those who have never lived as monks. But it can seem that by being in the choir for office we are achieving nothing, and – especially if we are not the world's greatest singers – we might suppose that really we would accomplish more by being somewhere else. The school, the parish, the retreat house – anywhere.

There is, in fact, a vital significance in the community being physically together in the same place at the key moments of our lives. A former abbot of my own community used to say that attendance at office was the way each monk gave himself to the brethren. Certainly in common prayer the monk tries to give himself to God, but there is an important sense in which we are giving ourselves to one another in these times – supporting one another's prayer, simply being there because presence matters. Monks go to God together, and are the vehicles of grace to one another, just as spouses are. The parallel is very far from exact, but there are common features. It was such an experience of the power of the presence of monks to one another that gave me the insight I needed to enter religious life.

When I was a university student, I went on retreat to a Benedictine monastery in Sussex. On the first day of my visit, I waited in the monastery church in the early morning, watching the play of light as the sun rose and the warm colours of the brick walls emerged from the secret darkness. As I watched the monastery church welcome the day, a single monk silently took his place in the choir seats behind the altar. The flowing black of his cowl, the Benedictine choir vestment, contrasted with the ochres and golds the morning light was picking out around the church. He was joined by another cowled figure, and then by others. While the community gathered there was the deepest silence around the building, an atmosphere of expectancy. The uniform black of the monks' cowls, their silent presence together, the sense of anticipation, all gave rise to the feeling that something was coming into being – the community had a palpable identity, and as the monks rose to their feet and Lauds began, it was evident that its purpose was praise. I knew then that I belonged in that choir.

The way the community gathers in choir is a powerful symbol of the overarching purpose for which it has gathered, and even before a word is said or sung, the physical presence of the brethren has a power that can hardly be understated. The *Rule* makes it abundantly clear that the monks' attitudes to one another are of the essence: 'No one is to pursue what he judges better for himself, but instead what he judges better for someone else. To their fellow monks they show the pure love of brothers' (RB72). Monks need one another.

The key to finding our way, then, is the ability to see. Baldly stated, it appears obvious – 'Where there is no vision, the people perish', as the Book of Proverbs tells us. But we have seen that it can be easy for us to ignore this fact and accept our society's deep distrust of what one former American president called 'the vision thing'. Should this happen, we can find that we have lost the sense of how to find our way. Where there should be a joyful drawing out, a calling forth and responding, we encounter only a dour plodding on. Even when we dignify such a trudging with that noble word 'perseverance' we cannot disguise the fact that the essence of what should be happening is missing.

Imagination is the key to the events that transform us. In this area, as in so many, we can be short-changed by an impoverished definition, and find ourselves lacking the crucial categories that would allow us to understand what is happening to us. In religious contexts, imagination is frequently equated with whimsy, and treated as the ultimate act of subjective self-indulgence. But there is a vast difference between indulging in fantasy and exercising our imagination.

It would be accurate to describe Einstein's achievement of the theory of relativity as one of the greatest modern exercises of creative imagination. It was imagination that allowed Crick and Watson to describe the double helix of DNA, the biological building block of all life. At the root of modern science stands the crucial theory of gravity which Isaac Newton grasped in one leap of imaginative insight. These examples from the supposedly 'hard-edged' world of science point to the power of imagination, and give the lie to any suggestion that imagination takes us away from reality into mere subjectivity. Of course, each of these scientists needed to be a skilled mathematician, to possess an extensive knowledge of the fact base of his specialism, and to spend many long hours in the testing out of alternative possibilities. Nevertheless, it was not these skills or aptitudes alone that broke new ground. It was the visionary quality we call imagination: the capacity to 'catch the marvellous'.

British theatre director Peter Brook in his book *The Empty Space* presents a series of approaches to what he terms 'the deadly theatre', a theatre where imagination has died. He argues that while life and death can be clearly identified in the human body, the onset of the moribund is much less clearly discernible in ideas, attitudes or cultural forms. He gives an example from classical French drama. 'One [deadly way of playing classical tragedy] is traditional, and this involves using a special voice, a special manner, a noble look and an elevated musical delivery.' In this 'deadly theatre' everything is done in 'what seems like the proper way . . . just as they are supposed to be in the best of classical theatres'. [10] But the reality is that we, the audience, are excruciatingly bored. Crucially, this theatre gives no life – we learn nothing.

I cannot read Brook's account of the 'deadly theatre' without thinking of liturgies I have attended where imagination has died. Just as Brook suggests in theatre, 'deadly liturgy' appears to fulfil all the requirements of the rubrics, and has been diligently prepared. But there is no fire, nothing is burning within us as we participate. The symbols remain merely the physical objects they always were, they open no doors into the sacred.

Just like our liturgy, our spiritual lives can be afflicted by the disease of a mere formalism. 'Deadly spirituality' is widespread. We have all experienced it. This is a faith in which the so-called truth, far from setting us free has imprisoned us, emptied our lives of everything that makes them worth living and left us as liabilities to ourselves and others. 'Deadly spirituality' is a way of approaching the life of prayer that can suggest that grim determination is the crucial quality that takes us across the crossroads and up the steep hills. If we were in a Hollywood film we might term this quality 'True Grit', and there certainly are those who see such an attitude as heroic.

But in fact this is a version of spirituality that treats people as somewhat akin to computers: each morning we 'boot up' – a process that acquired its name from the fact that it reminded the first users of the PC of the (impossible) act of pulling oneself up by the bootstraps – and then we chug along for the rest of the day carrying out the routines and programmes of the religious life. Perfection might be said to consist in achieving the lowest possible number of error statements. There is a peculiar capacity in religious people to fall into this pattern of life. Unfortunately, my experience of those who think they are computers is that, like their electronic idols, they tend to crash.

In 'deadly spirituality' what we have lost is the juiciness of the real. The squelchy, messy, zestful experience of biting into a piece of fruit. The engagement of our senses, the stirring of our hearts, even the stirring of our loins. Sometimes chaotic, sometimes confusing, but tantalising and true in a way that does not let go.

The reclaiming of the landscape of life must begin with finding the footprints of the ox in the places and spaces of our everyday. This activity involves a use of symbolic imagination. This imagination is in need of guidance, nourishment and nurturing. It works best not when we attempt to tread the path of the solitary genius, but when we inhabit a living community of faith, when we 'drink from our own wells'. A Hindu proverb has it that 'when the disciple is ready, the guru will appear', and we will often find that it is the very ground beneath our feet that shows the clearest trace of the ox's passing. But a further difficulty faced by many people in our modern world is that we do not find it easy to entrust ourselves to one another in this way. We do not want to be tied down.

We are frequently told that we live in an age that doubts the wisdom, perhaps even the possibility, of commitment. At the same time, we can see a profound yearning for the values of community in the society of our times: the stability and sense of identity, the rootedness, that is so often lacking for those who live in the modern city. As Simone Weil puts it, 'To be rooted is perhaps the most important and least recognised need of the human soul.'[11] Lacking a trust in the essential commitments we would like to believe in, but finding no other path to follow, can be a dispiriting descent into a nihilistic wilderness. Paradoxical as it may seem, only when we are rooted have we really begun to take risks.

As the experience of spending time in a monastic choir makes immediately apparent, monks are one of the clearest signs in the contemporary church of the reality of commitment. The vowed life, the patterned, regular way of living, the stability of a group in one place over time – in a world in which every involvement becomes provisional, in which the individual is all too often only the sum of her economic parts, these are signs of something we all say that we want.

Nevertheless, we fear this commitment. It is no accident that people of our time prefer to keep their options open. The 'deadly theatre' that we see all around us – the relationships we know to be sham, the ruts we see ourselves and others slipping into, the numbing routine in dead-end situations – all these realities frighten us, as well they might. Commitment is a response, not an initiative. Unless there is something that evokes from us a desire to be committed we will never be able to make that leap. Underpinning all commitments by men and women is the belief that God is committed to us. We can see all too clearly that in the absence of the rising sun of salvation, we do not have the confidence to leap on our own.

The tragedy is that commitment, far from limiting our options, opens up ways to travel that simply are not there until the commitment is made. As we stand on a threshold, we may think that we know what waits for us beyond the door, but the fact is that we do not. A friend who has taken the plunge into beginning his own business straight from university pointed out to me the following remarkable passage. It comes from a mountaineer, W. H. Murray, and was written in 1951 about an expedition to the Himalayas.

'We had definitely committed ourselves and were halfway out of our ruts. We had put down our passage money – booked a sailing to Bombay. This may sound too simple, but it is great in consequence. Until one is committed, there is hesitancy, the chance to draw back, always ineffectiveness. Concerning all acts of initiative (and creation), there is one elementary truth the ignorance of which kills countless ideas and splendid plans: that the moment one definitely commits oneself, then providence moves too. A whole stream of events issues from the decision, raising in one's favour all manner of unforeseen incidents, meetings and material assistance, which no man could have dreamt would have come his way.' [12]

Murray goes on to commend a view he attributes to the German poet Goethe: 'Whatever you can do or dream you can, begin it. Boldness has genius, power and magic in it!'

It is this visionary sense of commitment that we touch every morning in the prayers of Lauds. We reaffirm our sense that God is at work in the people and events of our lives, that we can learn to see this purpose, and that by responding to his call we engage in a journey of transformation. Commitment is the quality that empowers and generates possibilities.

To begin, to commit to the journey, is to become a real rebel in a society that misconstrues rebellion as conformity to prevailing moods and tradition as what happened yesterday. We are frequently presented with the view that commitment restricts freedom. In reality, it can do the very opposite. There is something immensely refreshing about being a beginner.

There is something of this eternal beginner in all of us if we are really alive. According to Zen Master Suzuki, the 'beginner's mind' is a vital quality in any spiritual seeker. 'In Japan we have the phrase *shoshin*,' he tells us, 'this means beginner's mind . . . In the beginner's mind there are many possibilities, in the expert's mind there are few'. [13]

To commit to something, we have to be prepared to see in new ways. We cannot begin something if we think we already know all there is to be learned. The beginner is a wonderful image of the person in whom God's spirit is at work, because no beginner believes they have attained something. The beginner sets out to encounter possibility, change, development. The beginner sets no limits. A beginner is pure potentiality.

This is the most important lesson of making a choice, and, as Suzuki states, 'this is also the real secret of the arts: always be a beginner.' [14]

Suzuki points us towards the crucial lesson of the signposts in our landscape: always be a beginner, because the beginner is looking out for the signs along the way. He does not think he already knows, and remains willing and able to be surprised. There is something of what Jung might have called the 'puer eternus' in the person whose life has been marinated in the spirit of God, the 'eternal child' who is constantly capable of beginning again.

Can we be wholly changed into fire? Can we be born again? Jesus, in commending the attitude of children, has frequently been interpreted in a way that exploits the helplessness of children, leaving us with the impression that we are being told to do as we are told, follow the authority of the church. A wiser understanding is that of the child as beginner, as reservoir of all possibilities. Become as children: always be beginners.

Benedict certainly believed his monks to be children in this sense. He ends the seventy-three chapters of his Rule with this advice:

> 'Are you hastening towards your heavenly home? Then, with Christ's help keep this little rule that we have written for beginners. After that, you can set out for the loftier summits of the teaching and virtues we mentioned above, and under God's protection you will reach them.' (RB73)

3

Into the Labyrinth

Midday Prayer

. . . doubt wisely; in strange way
To stand inquiring right, is not to stray;
To sleep, or run wrong, is. On a huge hill,
Cragged and steep, Truth stands, and he that will
Reach her, about must and about must go,
And what the hill's suddenness resists, win so.

John Donne, 'Satire 3'[1]

THE LANDSCAPE OF THE SPIRIT can look simple if we trace it
out with our fingers on someone else's map. After setting out,
the pilgrim (always the 'one who would valiant be') travels
through a variety of tribulations, achieves victories and suffers
setbacks, but ultimately presses on to the final goal – the heavenly
Jerusalem. Whether the map in question uses the language of a
journey to the celestial city, a ladder joining earth and heaven,
progress through the interior castle of the soul, or an ascent of
the holy mountain, both popular religious imagery and the
theology of the spiritual life can give the impression of a straightforward unilinear progress – the journey, difficult as it is, is a
one-way, forward movement towards the clear goal of the beatific
vision. Even classic accounts of the life of prayer handed on to us
from the great spiritual pilgrims of the past can give this
impression, with their language of successive and mutually
complementary states such as the purgative, illuminative and
unitive ways.

But the lived landscape of the soul turns out not to be like that. Not in the least goal-oriented, frequently pitted and potholed, traversed by crevasses, this is no steady plateau, but a craggy terrain of frightful, sheer mountains: here we may even encounter the 'cliffs of fall' so memorably described by the Jesuit poet, G. M. Hopkins.[2] And there is no simple map, unless perhaps — we might begin to think — it is the childhood snakes and ladders board, with its abrupt reversals and extraordinary rapid progressions. To tread the landscape of the spirit, we discover, is no simple pilgrim's progress, but is to enter a labyrinth, and it is not unusual for things to go wrong.

Faith leads us into a process of constant change, an ebbing and flowing movement into a mystery that lies always just beyond us. This imagery for our journey is more feminine than masculine, more circular than linear, more organic than mechanistic. No longer one way but iterative, the labyrinth is the place where experiences repeat, paths interweave, there are interruptions as patterns form and shift. In the monastic round of daily and seasonal worship, especially, we find that John Donne's image of the traveller who 'about must and about must go' rings more true than the attractive but misleading notion that we are constantly moving forward towards the clear and single goal. There are pauses and oases along the way. Oftentimes we circle around, and frequently go into reverse. There are 'stop' signs, and diversions are common. It is not unusual for the path to disappear completely, or for the straight route to slip right out from under the traveller's dangling feet. This is especially true at the mid-point of the journey.

Noon is symbolically the crisis point of the day, the moment of change when the bright morning of our innocence gives way to the more nuanced textures of an afternoon ripening towards experience. Monastics celebrate this moment by gathering once again in choir. We leave aside the immediate and often pressing needs of the day and, in Donne's phrase, 'stand inquiring'.

The monastic office for the middle of the day is brief and simple: but there is a large, clear 'stop' signal here, which halts the sometimes frenzied flow of activity. This moment of prayer acts to create a breakwater in the fast flowing day. Before things become so busy that we are carried away we make the conscious decision to pause, to consider where we are and what we are doing. Monastic life is, in fact, full of stop signs. According to St Benedict, we need them to warn us against hurtling into forgetfulness.

I remember, as a newcomer to the monastery, listening to a junior monk telling a group of visitors about the monastic day. He sketched a picture of an integrated day of work, prayer and community living, in which all the parts fitted neatly together. A refrain of 'and then we go into church and sing some more psalms' punctuated the account. Even as a novice I sensed that the picture presented was not quite right, but it took me twenty years of living the monastic life to work out what was wrong with it. The point is that the monastic day is not seamless: it is full of interruptions. Far from being a weaving together of disparate elements into a coherent whole, it is a patterning together of jagged, rough edges. There is indeed a pattern, but it is woven into a tapestry made from interruptions, none of them more intrusive than this common prayer at midday.

At the busiest time of the working day, when professional demands can be most acute, a monastic community steps aside from the bustle and sings the psalms: those sometimes passionate, sometimes desperate songs.

To anyone absorbed in the tasks of the professional world this lunchtime of flowing grief, joy and dismay – when monks momentarily sideline the workaday world – can appear anything from enviable, through unintelligible, to irresponsible, perhaps all of these. From the other side of the monastery wall, sometimes I simply envy those who are heading off to relax over a chatty lunch. Maybe the unexamined life has its advantages, I find myself thinking.

More than any of the other times of common prayer during the day, this midday moment asks us to stop and consider the route we have been following. Where is it taking us? Pausing momentarily, we may recognise that, as we hurried along, we actually missed the main path and have plunged into a labyrinth of byways. At midday we consciously turn to the wilderness experience of old testament Israel: travelling towards the land of promise, but finding the route circuitous and the path more taxing than could ever have been imagined – if, indeed, it is the correct path at all.

The Desert Fathers of Egypt identified noonday as a particularly active time for the demons. It is the specially favoured time for a vice they termed 'accidie' – a form of sour restlessness – which was regarded as the demon of the noonday *par excellence*. It is easy to see where they got this idea. Midday stands as the signpost marking those noonday demon times when questions arise, when confidence falls away, the path seems lost, and crisis intervenes. This mood of circling pointlessness, in which nothing we have been or done engages us any longer, places before us the temptation of supposing that the answer is to give up, to let it all go.

As the midday office prayer reminds us, this is the hour when Christ 'mounted the wood of the cross for our redemption'. We have travelled some way, crossed the wilderness and even reached the borders of the promised land, only to hear a rumour that 'This is a land that devours its inhabitants' (Numbers 13:32), and realise that we may need to turn back and retrace our steps. Where paths had appeared clear and straight, all at once there is confusion and reversal.

A medieval Carthusian Prior, Guigo, likens our situation to that of someone nostalgically missing a favourite piece of music. He tells us that we have become attached to just one of the phrases of what he calls 'the great song', and so we are upset when the wise singer continues his singing, moving on from the melody we loved and introducing new material into the performance. 'The one phrase you loved is taken from you and others succeed in their order. For he does not sing to you alone, or in accordance with your wishes, but his. The phrases which come after are unacceptable to you because they displace the one you loved in the wrong way.' [3] We may intuitively respond positively to Guigo's lovely image, and want to flow with the changing shape of the song. But the reality can be less than lyrical.

I found myself less well prepared for the noontime's ground-breaking moment when directions can change than for any other that I have faced. While most of what I have learned in twenty years of monking has been learned gradually, almost imperceptibly, this was different. My confusion was a force so great that it blew me right off the path I had supposed was solid beneath me.

It was an Internet website created by a young Canadian that planted the bomb under my cosy path: a site on which a native of Toronto had recorded, week by week over a period of two or three years, his discovery of who he was and what he wanted from his life.

I stumbled upon this online journal by chance, unaware that such a form of autobiography – unique to the world of electronic communication – even existed. Reading the journal hit me with an explosive impact.

Alternately brash and charming, always energetically audacious, the words of this twenty-one-year-old who called himself Aaron seized my attention. I found myself caught up in the tale he told of his journey into life as thoroughly as Coleridge's wedding guest, buttonholed by the Ancient Mariner. Enthralled, I rode the roller coaster of his words through the high and low points of his world. With him I cried, raged, fell in and out of love, laughed, lusted, hurt and healed. Someone I had never met reached out across thousands of miles and over a good twenty-year age gap and churned up parts of me I had forgotten were even there.

When the ride was over, this intimate stranger was as far away as he had ever been. But I found that I was no longer in the place from which I had begun. Coleridge's wedding guest is 'a sadder and a wiser man'[4] after his voyage with the Mariner. For me, it was as if earth movers had been at work. My solid ground had been torn apart. The landscape now had new places. Depths in my life had been uncovered, surfaces buried, the views and aspects of everyday had changed. What had been comfortingly familiar had become merely banal. My immediate surroundings appeared a monochrome monument to compromise and complacency, while in the distance new horizons beckoned, beguiling in their clarity and energy.

I did not understand my reaction. I had read autobiographies before, but never with this outcome. What was different this time?

There was a raw honesty in this young man, there was passion in his search for fulfilment, the magnetic quality of his personality shone out; but it was the sheer scale and vigour of his living that had seized my attention. His life seemed to be in technicolour, while mine was in black and white; his had three dimensions, mine only two. He was living alternately at vertiginous heights and shattering depths; I had opted for the safety of a steady middle ground.

I was reminded of the Liverpool housewife Shirley Valentine (the central character in the film of the same name), who laments in one climactic scene of her middle years the broken dreams she sees before her:

> What I kept thinking about was how I'd lived such a *little* life. And one way or another even that would be over pretty soon. I thought to myself, my life has been a crime really – a crime against God, because . . . I didn't live it fully. I'd allowed myself to live this little life when inside me there was so much. So much more that I could have lived a bigger life with – but it had all gone unused, an' now it would never be.[5]

Like Shirley's, mine now seemed 'such a little life', and I wept. I had never felt such confusion. Here I was, a supposedly mature man of forty-something, a responsible professional, a priest, consumed with the sense that I had missed out on some 'bigger life'. Somehow, twenty years had passed, and I had done nothing with them. Now I discovered that I was deeply fascinated by and even jealous of, someone who appeared to embody everything I had never been, and had never thought I wanted to be. Aaron was in almost every way my antithesis, but at that moment it was my antithesis that I wanted to be. 'I didn't know what I was doing', I heard myself say of my life choices. And I realised that this was true.

Could it be that there comes for all of us a moment when everything we have hoped for and striven towards is found empty of meaning, and it seems that only in the distance, beyond the rainbow, can purpose still be found? Like a conversion experience in reverse: sudden and dramatic for some, gradual and in almost indiscernible stages for others, meaning leeches away and only the dried-out husk is left behind. When this happened to me, I realised that nothing, literally nothing, had prepared me for this moment. I did not know that it was coming, no one had warned me, and I did not know what to do with it. A massive 'stop' sign stood in the road ahead of me, and I had no way of seeing whether there was a path to take me past this signpost.

In the *Divine Comedy* Dante's journey to paradise begins at the midday, midlife point where his earthly path gets lost:

> Midway this way of life we're bound upon
> I woke to find myself in a dark wood
> Where the right road was wholly lost and gone.[6]

I had read these lines many times, but had never supposed that they referred to a life experience, or that there would come a moment for me when the path would vanish. Dante discovered that the only route available to him from the dark wood took him in a wholly unexpected direction – not onward, or even backward, but *down*. Dante travels down into the depths of the Inferno, to confront the darker possibilities of the human heart. In some sense, it seems he too discovered his life had been two-dimensional, that there were depths he had not explored.

After a night of fitful sleep, I woke remembering a dream: something that it is rare for me to do. I had dreamed that I climbed through a trapdoor *down* into a derelict basement beneath my bedroom. Hardly a remarkable journey by Dante's standards, but in the waking world there is no basement beneath my bedroom. My dream basement was a neglected lumber room, filthy, damp and dark. Decaying storage crates were draped in dirty dustsheets, some of which had burst and were spilling their contents across the floor. It was clear from the spiders' webs and dust that no one had entered this area for a long time, and that if it was to be reclaimed as part of the house, there was a lot of work to do. Could it be that there was some connection between this 'new dimension' in my dream and the feelings I was experiencing? Was this basement my modern suburban image of Dante's medieval hell?

The dream image of a neglected lumber room in the basement proved to be an invitation to enter the spiritual lost-property department, to reclaim the aspects of myself that I was neglecting or putting to one side. It was a film that gave me this clue to my dream, and in doing so began the process of helping me to understand what had happened to me as I read Aaron's life story.

There is a striking moment in Anthony Minghella's film 'The Talented Mr Ripley' in which the eponymous anti-hero, Tom Ripley, explains how he deals with the psychological weight of being a murderer. 'Don't you put the past in a room, in the cellar, and lock the door and just never go in there? Because that's what I do,' he tells us. 'Then you meet someone special and all you want to do is toss them the key and say *open up, step inside,* but you can't because it's dark and there are demons and if anyone saw how ugly it was . . .'[7]

I realised that, like Minghella's character I had gone through life putting into a deep, dark room the emotions and experiences, the aspects of myself, I didn't want to deal with. I too was adept at closing the door and walking away. Perhaps the contents of my basement were less lurid than those of Ripley: nevertheless the spiritual and emotional lost property does not sit quietly. It has a way of rising up again, cluttering our tidy hallways at the moments we least expect it. What has lain in the neglected basement breaks through the polished surface of our lives, tripping us up and forcing a change of direction.

It dawned upon me that, by one of those bizarre coincidences that Jung termed 'synchronicity', at the moment I needed to meet him someone had appeared who embodied many of the life choices I had not made. Perhaps I had glimpsed fragments of my neglected self in other contexts, but I realised that in reading about Aaron's life I had been reading about my own shadow self, and had discovered the extraordinary fascination of 'the path not taken'. What was tormenting me was not a fixation with someone else, but a rediscovery of myself. The person whose story I had read on the Internet was *me*.

'Midway this way of life we're bound upon' we must each wake to our need to address dimensions of ourselves we have been neglecting. What Aaron's life story awoke in me was the world of feeling, and especially the need for love. I had thought I was pursuing this through the religious life, but I was, in fact, ignoring it. Jungian psychologist Marie-Louise von Franz identifies the neglect of love – the feeling dimension of life – as the central dilemma of western culture. In place of a fully embodied, passionate loving, she claims, we have accepted mere sentimentality. This soppy niceness is love robbed of its visceral energy. Meanwhile, the neglected energy of Eros, confined to the cellars of our personalities, awaits its opportunity to break out: 'the more sentimental love is, the more brutal is its shadow following behind it.' [8]

The strange and terrifying Bluebeard story, with its bloody chamber, tyrant husband and murdered brides, can help us to understand this suppression of the shadow. The tale concerns the nobleman's newly-wed wife who unlocks and enters the one chamber of his castle that had been explicitly forbidden to her. Inside the chamber, she discovers the entombed remains of his previous wives, each of them murdered by the man she has just married.

If we read the story symbolically, recognising that we ourselves are both the husband and the brides, it is possible to identify a way of living in which we are each the Bluebeard of our own lives: at every junction of the path we follow we have abandoned ('murdered') dimensions of ourselves. In childhood, in youth and as adults we have dispatched to the bloody chamber first our physical selves, then our emotions, and finally, perhaps, even our critical intellect. The deep, hidden chamber of the castle has filled up with corpses. Eventually, some part of ourselves will stumble upon this hidden room, and threaten to bring back into the light those aspects of our experience that have been entombed. This is the moment of crisis faced by so many individuals in the noonday of their lives. The bloody chamber is opened. And then, to update Dante's claim about the need to explore the Inferno, 'all hell breaks loose', as it must if we are to become whole people once again.

Monastic spirituality, I now know, recognises this need of constantly opening our bloody chambers to the noonday sun of grace. It took a casual meeting in cyberspace with an unknown Canadian journal writer to make me see it.

The Desert Fathers told the story of how a high-ranking courtier from the city of Alexandria travelled to the hermitages of Scete to visit a renowned elder. Each day for three days the visitor attempted to engage the monk in talk about spirituality and theology, but although he received the courtier hospitably, the elder spoke not a word in reply. Embarrassed on the visitor's behalf, the hermit's young disciple asked his master why he would not speak to the Alexandrian. 'He asks me about heavenly matters,' replied the master, 'and I know nothing of such things.' Suddenly understanding what the elder was teaching by his silence, the disciple advised the courtier to attempt a different approach. 'You must speak to him of the passions of your soul,' the visitor was told. Swallowing his pride, the courtier approached the elder with an open heart, sharing the struggles, failures and sins he had never allowed anyone else to know. At once, he received the words he had been seeking.

We can hide the deepest parts of ourselves from the real work of the spirit of God behind a variety of barriers, but one of the most subtle of these – as this story brings home – is the language of spirituality itself. Instead of leading us into a fuller, more honest engagement with the whole of ourselves, with 'the passions of our soul', the discourse of theology and spirituality, even the process of prayer itself, can become a means of avoiding this encounter. This is the lesson the desert elder is teaching, and it was the lesson I was struggling to learn the hard way.

The issue here is not whether we are perfectly in tune with every dimension of ourselves at every moment, surely an impossible ideal, but whether there are aspects of our whole human experience we systematically refuse to recognise. Many elements of ourselves, especially the raw areas of our griefs and our vulnerability, issues linked to our sexuality or our need for intimacy and for friendship, can be genuinely difficult to face and even painful.

It is inevitable that, to a greater or lesser extent, we will fail fully to address some of these areas of life. The feelings that accompany crucial events can be simply too overwhelming to be worked through completely at the moment they first occur. Other experiences, of their very nature, ripple outwards across the surface of our lives and must be addressed many times in different ways as we grow older and wiser. We are, so to speak, our own labyrinth. Some kinds of feelings may fall into categories we have learned or been taught to regard as somehow dangerous or just plain wrong. But, whatever the reason, we travel through life trying to leave behind us dimensions of ourselves we have failed adequately to address, and these facets of ourselves, buried but not dead, refuse to go quietly.

The ultimate result of our repeated failures to untangle these emotional knots can be an alienation from the vital core of ourselves. Not at home in our own skins, we become, in effect, passengers in our own lives. We may be aware of discomfort, even of pain, but we are very likely to misidentify the source of the problem. We repeat the same mistake again and again, convinced that *this* time we will get it right. But with each crashing failure, we actually make the problem worse.

Fiction editor Rust Hills, advising writers on the creation of believable characters, identifies the phenomenon clearly: 'There's a kind of larger pattern of behaviour that people fall into; not just the day to day routine, but a sort of repetitious pattern to their whole lives . . . people try all sorts of ways to solve their problems and sometimes adopt a role that ought to be temporary or transitional, but then they get stuck that way. It's like when the needle gets stuck in one groove of the record – there's still sound and there's still movement; but the sound is senseless and the movement is somehow static, going around in circles . . . With new enthusiasm and firm resolve to break out of their maze, they waste their vitality by inevitably rushing into the same corridor as before, to make the choice that puts them right back where they were.' [9] When we are unknowingly at odds with ourselves, this hellish circling about seems to be our self-imposed penalty.

The process of losing touch with our deepest self begins with a dishonouring of our physical, embodied experiences. 'Within this fathom-long body is found all of the teachings', [10] the Buddha is reputed to have said. I was shocked to learn from Buddhist friends that they understood the Buddha to have been speaking literally, because it had not occurred to me the physical world could so fully encompass the economy of salvation. Perhaps when Jesus said we should direct our attention towards what 'comes from within a person' he meant attend to our bodies: he was after all a member of a culture that was more aware of the physicality of existence than are most modern westerners.

If our state of alienation from ourselves begins with a lack of awareness of our bodies, then a true spirituality must address this fact. We all need to listen to the wisdom that comes from our bodies, receiving our physical being as a gift. Sadly, many of us have perceived this gift as a burden, or even as a curse.

It may be that we lose touch with our physical selves because of events or experiences that make us uncomfortable with our bodies. Perhaps the chaos of adolescence would be the obvious place to look for the starting point of many such anxieties. Perhaps it is the discomfort with physical sexuality that many have claimed to find endemic to the Christian tradition. Our refusal to experience bodily sensations in their fullness could equally be related to a childhood which left us with a vague feeling that our bodies are objects of shame, or at least not so respectable as our minds.

But however and whenever our discomfort with our bodies begins, many of us will have found that our disregard for our physical selves was cemented into place by a false spirituality. An example would be the widespread assumption that in the New Testament 'the flesh' means the body and 'the spirit' means the mind. Whatever this distinction meant to biblical authors, it certainly is not the same as the modern distinction between mind and body. Despite this fact, many contemporary religious people could justly be accused of living almost exclusively in their heads: in many of us the flesh has become word again.

Closely linked to our discomfort with our physical being is the confusion that many of us who try to live lives of spiritual dedication can feel with the profound, chaotic world of our emotions, especially the unpredictable dimension of our sexual desire. From earliest childhood, the attitudes we have internalised towards our emotions were being stored up. It may be that we were always told that 'boys don't cry' or 'nice girls aren't jealous', or perhaps we were surrounded by role models who did not help us to learn appropriate ways of handling, for example, our anger or our desire. Allowing ourselves to realise that we had certain feelings may have led us into situations that hurt us, leaving a sense that it was the feeling that caused the hurt.

As a result, when we encounter the Christian tradition of prayer, we may find in it something it does not contain: the idea that prayer involves the suppression both of our bodies and of our feelings. To take but one example: Gregory the Great writes of our busy inner world, so distracted at the moment of prayer that 'the prostrate spirit is ignominiously trodden by the feet of a crowded market place. The soul which is disordered by a rabble riot of sensations and thoughts suffers, as it were, from overpopulation.' [11] It is only too easy to hear him telling us to flee from, to suppress, the physical feelings, powerful emotions or complex ideas that make us uncomfortable.

Eventually, we can build for ourselves a positively Manichaean spirituality: the physical sensations of our bodies and the insistent demands of our emotional world are 'of the flesh' and to be resisted; only the pure and godly imaginings of our minds are 'of the spirit' and to be pursued. We will leave behind the confusion and humiliation of embodied feelings, choosing instead a calm, straight road to paradise that we identify with the way of Christian prayer. But this is to treat spirituality less as the 'royal road' to heaven described by the fathers of the church – for whom the life of the spirit certainly involved a willingness to engage with the self in all its fullness – than as a species of urban bypass, set up to avoid the embarrassment of a rundown town centre. We conceive of the spiritual life precisely as a way of avoiding the messiness of the business of living. We 'pray' so as not to hear the messages our body is sending, the calls of our feelings, and the perplexing demands of real human situations. But this is not Christian prayer, and it is not human living. Rather, we have become trapped in a totally cerebral mode of being. Imprisoned in the high tower of thought, we live as though we have been anaesthetised. Meanwhile, the dark cellar far below is filling up.

And so we can arrive at a deeply misguided form of spirituality that presents prayer as the solution to all problems. Jesus himself can be presented as the one who 'saves' us from the need to work through the experience of being physical, emotional, thinking beings. This is a misunderstanding that can be hard to identify, because calling a spade a spade in this area can look like a form of disloyalty to the faith community or even blasphemy. But prayer is not the solution to all problems, for the simple reason that it is not a means of escape. In fact, even when correctly understood, prayer is the *solution* to remarkably few problems – perhaps even none at all. That is not what it is for.

According to Abbot John Chapman, 'the more you pray the better it gets, the less you pray the worse it gets'.[12] Like most aphorisms, Chapman's dictum needs to be unpacked. If we are living in the alienated state I have been describing, following Chapman's advice could be the very worst thing we could do. Business gurus claim that a failing company will resist the need to rethink, to change, and will instead simply work harder on what it has always done. It will do even more of what has caused the problem in the first place. Likewise the seeker whose path is vanishing, in trying harder usually makes things worse. Multiplying our retreats and spiritual exercises simply takes us further from understanding ourselves and being able to change than we were before.

To some extent, all of us have been involved in this tearing apart of 'psychic opposites',[13] so that body and spirit, emotion and intellect, heaven and earth, have been set at odds; with God confined, disastrously, to one side of the equation and an impoverished notion of prayer employed to keep him there. As I became aware of this, I found that I had to recognise the inadequacy of my understanding of prayer, and even of the image of God that lay behind my understanding of prayer.

Whether we are offered an over-simple model of prayer or manage to generate it for ourselves probably does not matter. These issues are never clear-cut, nor is it helpful to attach blame to oneself or to others. What matters is that we realise that prayer can, all too easily, become a means to flee from the complex and demanding world of our physical experiences and emotions, not an engagement with that world. Ironically, it is the very idealism and dedication we bring to our religious life, the striving that makes possible the spiritual journey, that can lay us open to this misunderstanding. Only someone to whom prayer and the quest for God really matter will make this mistake.

Once I saw I had ignored my real feelings, I needed to mourn and to grieve as I had never done before. I had never consciously tried to hide from myself the fact that, in entering dedicated religious life and embracing celibacy, I was excluding the possibility of a lifetime's intimate personal relationship with one other person. I had not ignored the fact that I would never have children. Nor had I knowingly refused to recognise that, at times, I experienced these realities as loss. But I had never allowed myself to touch, until this moment, the depth of this loss. Some theologies of celibacy characterise the state as one of 'radical incompleteness'; the celibate, in this view, is a sign of the incompleteness of all humanity until our hearts rest in the one for whom they were created. I am sure this is true; but until now I had not felt the awful power of that term 'radical'.

The imagery occasionally encountered of God as the 'spouse' of the celibate religious may be fine at some level of discourse, but in almost every way that matters it is desperately misleading. God is no use in bed. God does not hold you when you are down. He does not take you clubbing, to the cinema, or cook you a meal. He doesn't smell good and feel warm beside you. Examples could be multiplied, but the point is clear enough. I had chosen not to have these experiences, and suddenly I needed to mourn the life that had not been. The longing to share intimately with a partner had been speaking loudly in me, but I had refused to hear. At some level of myself I had felt it wrong or too dangerous to allow myself to know what I was feeling. Into the dark room with that set of emotions. Above all, ignore that physical longing.

As these feelings obtruded more and more into my conscious experience, I rediscovered the gift of tears. There were days when my emotions shifted like the English weather, and from one hour to the next either sunshine or a cloudburst might be imminent. But the most extraordinary discovery of this grieving was the release of energy that followed from it. Far from being an end, it was a beginning.

First, there came a new acceptance of the woundedness of my humanity. We can all acknowledge notionally that human woundedness is not a weakness, but in some way or other a strength: 'O happy fault, O necessary sin'. Experiencing this, living it, is another matter. Most of the cultural, social and personal influences that bear upon us communicate a different message. It is deeply alien to most of the lessons we have learned about how to survive in life – the brave face, the stiff upper lip. But St Paul is surely correct: when we are weak, then we are strong.

I had come to recognise that some opportunities had passed me by and would never come again. I had made choices, and not every consequence of those choices has been easy to live with. But there was no purpose to burying that realisation. As soon as I allowed myself to feel the hurt I had been hiding, healing could begin.

The paradoxical fact is that the only strength we can have comes from our God-given, graced and wounded human nature. If we fight this, we cut away the very branch we sit on. It seems as though the emotional effort required to maintain an illusion of wholeness is considerable. And who, in the end, are we trying to fool? Mostly ourselves. When the pretence is dropped and the wound is acknowledged there is a sense of freedom and of peace. No, we are not whole: but then we do not try to pretend that we are. With this change of perspective the problems do not go away, but the surroundings are different.

A wound, symbolically, is an opening, and an opening is a way to new possibilities. We are offered the gift of vulnerability – the walls are shattered, the defences are broken down. With new eyes we look more honestly at who and what we are. As we step beyond fear we accept the gift of authenticity, entering a path which cannot be actively sought but only accepted as gift. At this moment I am offered the gift of being who I am, and I can accept others with a new depth of understanding of who they are.

And from this follows the second dimension of growth that I discovered: I am not alone. Almost from the moment that I admitted to myself the extent of my woundedness, I found myself surrounded by a 'great cloud of witnesses' who had already begun to explore this dimension of themselves. The admission to myself that I was needy and hurting brought about not a solution to the problem, but a new context for addressing it: the company and support of new friends or of old friends encountered in new ways. The greatest of ironies is that as we open up our hearts to recognise our loneliness, we discover that we are no longer lonely. Instead, we help each other and live as shelter for each other. The firm root of friendship has hold of our hearts.

I discovered a new gratitude for and commitment to my religious brethren. I was able to share with them and receive their love and support in a way I had not experienced before.

I was losing, finally, my fear of living and feeling. I began to meet God in my encounters with others. I discovered depths of feeling in myself that I had not allowed myself to notice. Above all, I realised that in these chaotic emotions, disturbing as they frequently were, God was at work. Like Jacob, I found that 'the Lord was in this place, and I knew it not' (Genesis 28).

The action of God in moments of chaos can no more be invoked than it can be predicted or prevented. 'Asked or unasked, God will come', as the motto outside Jung's consulting room read. Biblical images of God – shepherd, farmer, lover – always make God the one who is active. He takes the initiative. It is disconcerting, though, to be on the receiving end of this activity. And this is another area where the maps of our seeking can be misleading – they assume that we are the searchers. Yet God is the seeker, and we are the object of the search. This is the strangest lesson of all.

The crisis moment at the midpoint of our life's journey is fraught with peril: not for nothing does Gary Cooper's Sheriff Will Kane confront his nemesis at 'High Noon', accompanied by the tacky old lyric, 'Do not forsake me, O my darling'. Monastic life is usually less melodramatic, but the monk's profession prayer 'Support me, Lord, as you have promised, and I shall live; do not disappoint me of my expectation' expresses a sentiment that is not so very dissimilar. The Desert Fathers thought of the monastic drama as a process of purification, a burning away of dross akin to the smelting of gold in a furnace. They used the biblical story of the three young men in the furnace from the book of Daniel as an image of the crisis they knew we had each to undergo: plunged into the turbulent fires, baked like bread in an oven, we find that we are walking alongside others and accompanied by one who 'looks like a son of the gods'.

To recognise in our reversals the moments when we move forward may appear the most bizarre of attitudes. But no other reading of the noonday crisis makes more sense. The 'stop' sign stands before us. It can halt all progress, shattering and unravelling our world. It marks a perilous place.

But it can also cause us to turn back from danger, and discover that our view of the journey was wrong. 'To turn, turn, will be our delight,' goes the old Shaker hymn, 'till in turning, turning, we come round right.' The landscape through which we have been travelling may seem to have taken us nowhere, or even moved us back to somewhere we supposed we had already visited. But these turns were necessary. We will not end up simply dizzy, but will find instead that the shape of the pilgrimage was not the one we had expected.

The prayer tradition of walking a labyrinth has helped many travellers to understand these paradoxes in their journey. Cut into the turf of green valleys, built into the floors of cathedrals, or set out in rough stones in quiet fields, the labyrinth is a valuable tool for considering this midday stage of the Christian journey.

Many of our contemporaries are rediscovering this ancient prayer form, and deriving great insight from it.

Christians appear first to have used the prayerful walking of a symbolic labyrinth-shaped path in the medieval period, when it became an understandably popular alternative to the dangerous and expensive pilgrimage to Jerusalem. Today, labyrinths are painted onto large sheets of canvas and laid out in chapels, or marked out on the lawn with ropes and pegs. Wherever they are found, they exercise a magnetic fascination. A labyrinth, in one tradition of thought, is a symbolic image not simply of pilgrimage in the geographical sense, but of the journey we each make through life: a journey to the centre, a return to the heart. The labyrinth path, which 'about must and about must go', vividly expresses the reversals and crises of the journey that this chapter has explored.

The labyrinth is not a maze: labyrinths have only one path, whereas mazes have many paths and dead ends. The maze will present us repeatedly with the confusing possibility of being truly lost. The reversals of the labyrinth, by contrast, represent a very different experience. When the labyrinth's one path circles back upon itself, it seems as though we are approaching a dead end. But with the later perspective of seeing the whole pattern of the labyrinth it becomes clear that, however the path may twist, the journey will ultimately arrive at the centre.

The labyrinth can be undertook as a representation of our passage through the years and our life's experience. The turns and twists reflect the path of life, a journey which involves change and transition, rites of passage and even the cycles of nature. Walking the path of the labyrinth can show us that nothing is ever wasted: every step, however circuitous the path may seem, takes us closer to the end we seek.

One who wants to pray the labyrinth need only step onto the path and begin. This walking prayer is a gentle dance that requires no special skills or movements that call attention to themselves. The labyrinth allows the one who walks it to pray with the body, to be aware of the interplay of limbs and movement through space. In a way that threatens no one, we are allowed to experience ourselves as physical beings in a physical space. Our bodies are the vehicle and the means of our prayer – the cerebral nature of some prayer forms is helpfully side-stepped, allowing dimensions of ourselves to come into our prayer which might otherwise be left at the church door.

Our breathing, our quiet walking, the changing perspectives we see as the path moves us from one direction to another – any of these can form the focus of our attention. Some pray the labyrinth with a purpose – to solve a problem, to digest an issue, to hold a grief before God. At other times we can walk simple to find out where the journey takes us.

We travel through the labyrinth by weaving a path of recursive arcs, and as we do so the relentless demands of the many dimensions of our lives can be lifted from our shoulders. We move more naturally, because we no longer hurry – the turning about and about makes it pointless to rush frantically forward. It can seem that we are carried on the slowly swirling waters of a great stream which turns and eddies as we travel: a lazy movement which travels not onwards but down, and supported in this slowly turning pool we can feel safe to experience our own physical presence.

By touching our bodily presence, we touch our emotions. Hurts that we have neglected, joys that we have refused can be reclaimed. The process of crossing from one side of the labyrinth to the other can express in space the crossing from the conscious to the unconscious mind that we have been addressing earlier in this chapter. Not least among its gifts, the labyrinth can set free images from our dream life, those great symbols of our personal myth, allowing them to become part of that larger tale to which we all belong. As we walk the labyrinth, 'to turn, turn, will be our delight', and the reverses of our path are recognised as 'stop' signs no longer, nor as blank walls with no way through, but as necessary moments in a greater movement, phrases of the great song.

The recursive pattern of the monastic day was for me the labyrinth-like path I trod as I encountered the frightening midday moment of the journey. But on the other side of fear is illumination.

'I really don't know why I'm doing this,' one monk told another, speaking of the process of gathering to fling ancient lyrics at one another across empty spaces at odd times of the day: a process we usually call the Divine Office.

'Thank God,' replied his confrère.

It is at this moment of realisation that God has entered the labyrinth and walks alongside us.

4

Tincture and Reflection

Vespers (Evening Prayer)

What we are hangs upon that moment —
Which *will* come —
When the cross is taken in the warp
And the weave is certain.

On the drying-ground
Where the wet wools are hung to blow,
Scarlet, blue,
I was first aware of a true pattern

To do with light . . .
Jean Earle, 'The Woollen Mill'[1]

HIDDEN IN THE LATER CHAPTERS of the book of Jeremiah is a story that does not often get the audience it deserves. The prophet, whose task was so challenging both to himself and to his hearers that tradition has it he was put to death to silence his message, creates a scroll on which his prophetic words are written down. This scroll ultimately finds its way into the palace of the king of Judah, where it is read to the king.

> It was the ninth month, and the king was sitting in the winter house, and there was a fire burning in a brazier before him. As the secretary read three or four columns from the scroll the king would cut them off with a penknife and throw them into the fire in the brazier until

the entire scroll was consumed in the fire that was in the brazier.

(Jeremiah 36)

The spiralling parchment of the scroll, endlessly turning back upon itself, stands as a striking parallel to the spiral path of the labyrinth. Each of them can effectively symbolise the spirit's action in our lives: a recursive path as we travel further into the mystery. At the same time, the darker dimensions of Jeremiah's message, the wrath of God, judgement against his chosen people, are a clear instance of the shadow side of the divine action. To this challenge we do not readily grant a hearing. The king, like most of us, wants a straight path, not the disruptive 'turning, turning' of conversion that can throw everything into question. Thus he cuts away at the spiralling scroll and burns the powerful words of the prophet, just as we can each be guilty of cutting away whole dimensions of what life has brought our way, hoping thereby to burn away the memories we do not want to face. But, of course, in so doing we fail to hear the word that has been spoken in those events.

The Jeremiah scroll brings to mind a second biblical scroll, that of St John in the Book of Revelation:

> And I saw in the right hand of him who was seated on the throne a scroll written within and on the back, sealed with seven seals; and I saw a strong angel proclaiming with a loud voice, 'Who is worthy to open the scroll and break its seals?' And no one in heaven or on earth or under the earth was able to open the scroll or to look into it. Then one of the elders said to me, 'Weep not; lo, the lion of the tribe of Judah, the Root of David, has conquered, so that he can open the scroll and its seven seals.'
>
> (Revelation 5:1–5)

A sealed scroll, in the language of biblical imagery, contains the working out of God's plan in human lives. This plan, sealed because hidden from human knowledge, can be broken open – revealed to us – by Christ, the lion of the tribe of Judah.

In both stories, we are invited to understand the scroll as the text of our life, a text in which God writes, and which Christ allows us to read. The reading is a challenge we may find disconcerting – so much so that we can cut away much of the message that awaits us, preferring an attenuated account of who we are to the rich but complex reality. Equally significantly, as the New Testament passage makes clear, the scroll will remain sealed unless we have the courage to allow Christ to open it for us. We have found in earlier chapters that a false view can present itself to us: that of an illusory independence. A crucial breakthrough in discerning the true depths within our own lives comes when we are prepared to accept the reality of interdependence – the role that others play in enabling us to own aspects of ourselves – and above all the reality of salvation, which is a gift we are given, not an achievement we can boast of winning. When we attempt to discern the pattern we have woven through our lives, the same principles apply.

Late in the afternoon, as darkness falls in some months of the year, or – more often – with the light of the ripening sun spilling through the clerestory of the Abbey Church, the monastic community gathers to celebrate the evening office of Vespers. This is a moment that brings together the varied tasks and moods of the day. What has been, has been. The working day draws close to its end, and there remains a space to reflect and to give thanks. The evening brings a moment of sifting and settling, allowing the raw material of experience to begin to take on the shape it actually has, and speak its word to us.

The bright morning was the time of setting forth, and the rising sun summoned us to new challenges and deeds that might change the world. The morning was, so to speak, the assertively masculine section of the day, in which we followed the outer path of building, making and achieving. God spoke to us most clearly through the externals of our lives: the people around us, the situations we encountered, sign and symbol in the arts or in our religious observances. As we travelled, our ideals were formed and tested, and – if we were courageous enough – were put into practice. We began careers, established families, took on responsibilities. This was our time of doing.

Noon brought us to the disorienting moment of crisis, in which we discovered the cost of our morning's work. The turning point between morning and evening, the time that stands between the two worlds, midday presented a dangerous test to the values we thought we had clearly understood and built our lives upon. For many of us, the breakthrough to the afternoon of life occurred through a failure, a 'breakdown' of some kind, in which we could no longer see a clear way before us. Despair threatened to overwhelm the now fragile sense of ourselves that had appeared so secure. And so we found, by allowing the inner world we had so far ignored to begin its work in our outer lives, a new balance, a renewed energy. The light of the feminine, the inner energy, had begun to arise, and we knew for the first time that 'the kingdom of God is within you'. This was our time of questioning.

Now the evening brings a time to turn back from the fields and forests of our labours, back from the towns and cities of our toils, to the home, the hearth, and above all the heart. This is the inwardly directed time of assembling, sorting and shaping. Masculine and feminine begin to coalesce, and our task becomes the discerning of the shape we have made in all that has gone before.

This moment in the day calls us to slow down. To understand this landscape we must travel on foot – the fast-moving vehicles we prefer to utilise will hinder our progress. There is a sense in which we can prevent this process from happening precisely by trying *too* hard – something that can be a puzzle to our achievement-oriented culture. But this process of discerning the shape of what has been cannot be striven for – it is freely offered and, if we wish, we can choose to receive it.

The Russian Orthodox Archbishop Anthony Bloom used to tell a story that makes this point. An older member of his congregation came to see the Archbishop, who was widely (and rightly) regarded as an authority on Christian prayer. His visitor shared with Archbishop Anthony the concern that although she had prayed all her life, both in the public liturgy and often for hours in private devotions, she had never for a moment had any sense of the presence of God in her life. Were her prayers not heard? Was she not loved by the God to whom she was praying?

After talking with his visitor about her prayer practices and about her life in general, Archbishop Anthony offered her this advice: when you next come to your time of prayer, don't kneel, don't recite any prayers or psalms, but simply sit down in your favourite armchair by the fire, relax, and see what happens. Sure enough, the woman followed the Archbishop's guidance, and simply relaxed by the fire in her sitting room. A committed and busy person, she had not usually allowed herself the 'luxury' of time apparently wasted in this way. 'What a lovely room,' she reflected, as she looked about her at the ornaments, the furniture and the pictures that had accumulated in the many years she had lived in this house. She had never stopped to look at the room in this way before, but now she was suddenly aware of how blessed she was in the symbols of family and friendship that surrounded her. She was warmed by the fire, supported by the cushions of her chair, and delighted by the view from her window. Gratitude and joy for the richness of the life she had led were the emotions in her heart. Just as she had been instructed, she made no special effort to pray, but inevitably, she thanked God for all that this room and its contents represented to her. Gradually, she realised that it was as if she was listening to God speaking words of love to her – and every aspect of her life was one of those words, mediated to her by the physical contents of the room in which she was sitting.

Finally, it dawned upon her that this was what the Archbishop had intended to happen: she had been so busy in every dimension of her life that her busyness had carried over even into her prayer – she had talked to God, praised and thanked him, pleaded with him and complained to him, but never *listened* to him. Never had she stopped to allow her own life to become the word of God to her. This was what the Archbishop had discerned as he listened to her dismay, and his solution was to tell her to stop, to listen, to reflect.

Like the woman who visited Archbishop Anthony, I really only began to discover the reflective, receptive dimension of the

Christian journey when I was firmly but kindly told to take some time off each week. Like many a middle-aged man before me, I had convinced myself that the busier I became the more real I was. I have heard the problem called 'presenteeism' and also 'work-aholism'. But whatever name it goes by, the lifestyle preoccupied by achievement is not confined to the City or to the task of bringing up families – obsessive overwork can be found in religious life every bit as much as in the secular world. It is as if we become convinced that if we stop working, we will cease to exist. Of course, I had never articulated the situation to myself in such stark terms, but this was essentially my outlook.

At first, I interpreted any attempt to persuade me to look at the situation differently as a lack of appreciation for my work, a direct criticism of what I was doing. 'If you want me to do things differently, this must be because I'm doing things *wrong*; if you want me to work less, this must be because you don't *value* what I'm doing.' It takes real love to tell someone the truth in this kind of situation – because every strategy attempted will be thrown straight back at the friend, who will be accused of not caring for the one she is attempting to support. I took some while to see the real point that was being made: slow down, look around, take time to enjoy who you are.

'You mean, you just want me to take an evening off?'

'Yes, just that.'

This was some of the best advice I was ever given. An hour or two sitting quietly in a pleasant room, time to read or to see a film, and a slow, relaxing meal with a friend – simple and obvious strategies for reconnecting, but things I had to be more or less forced to do – kicking and screaming all the way – before I saw the way into the reflective stage of the journey.

A major factor that keeps us moving forward on the workaholic treadmill is the fear we can each experience of facing what lies within. Towards the end of Henrik Ibsen's drama of self-avoidance and self-discovery Peer Gynt the eponymous hero experiences a strange moment of epiphany. After a lifetime of travel and adven-ture he too turns back and looks within himself, finally asking the essential question: who am I? Peer actually finds what most of us only fear we will discover if we undertake this task. He peels an onion – a symbolic enacting of his desire to discover what lies at the core of his own life – only to discover that an onion does not have a core.

'I'm going to peel you now, my good Peer! You won't escape either by begging or howling.' He takes an onion and pulls off layer after layer. ' . . . What an enormous number of layers! Isn't the kernel soon coming to light? I'm blessed if it is! To the innermost centre, it's nothing but layers – each smaller and smaller. Nature is witty!'[2]

There is no human fear more profound than the fear that, in the end, we amount to nothing, have achieved nothing, mean nothing to anyone. We live with the daily terror that, at the core, there is quite simply nothing at all. And this is a fear that is shared by all of us, a fear that keeps us running, terrified of the moment of returning to the depths of ourselves – because we believe that, like Peer Gynt, we will look inside and discover emptiness. Peeling away the layers of our life we will encounter meaningless-ness, an empty core that threatens our sense of self-worth by presenting us with a plunge into the absurd.

The layers of the onion, the spirals of the scroll: we can join Peer Gynt or the Judean king in ignorantly cutting away the intricate pattern we have made of our lives, in which case we will leave ourselves with empty hands, or we can slow down, dare to stay still, and undertake the paradoxically demanding work of 'reading' the pattern, discovering a fullness of life we had hardly suspected.

As monks pray the psalms, we reflect with the psalmist on God's activity in the history of his people, Israel – the psalms call on us to 'remember' what the Lord has done. These historical psalms are only one of the many ways in which the Hebrew Bible attempts to understand God's nature and purpose by examining the nation's history. The prophets recall Israel's attentions to the lessons of God's ways in the past (not, as our modern use of the term to imply knowledge of the future might suggest, to what is to come). Historians and chroniclers attempt to find the pattern of God's purpose with his people by gathering tales of the past. In the Hebrew scriptures, the layers of the onion are treated not with casual disdain but with honour.

The gospels make clear that Jesus practised the same pondering over the sacred story as a way of understanding his own nature and mission, and as a way of explaining himself to his disciples. Memorably, he laments the slowness of heart of Cleopas and his companion when he joins them on the Emmaus road, 'And beginning with Moses and all the prophets, he interpreted to them in all the scriptures the things concerning himself' (Luke 24:27).

At the heart of the Office of Vespers is the Song of Mary, the Magnificat: 'My soul magnifies the Lord, and my spirit rejoices in God my saviour' (Luke 1). This New Testament Psalm is a reflection upon Israel's history that identifies and highlights specifically the action of God on behalf of the poor. Mary the mother of Jesus gives thanks that God has 'shown strength with his arm, he has scattered the proud . . . put down the mighty from their thrones, and exalted those of low degree.' Once again, we are invited to look back over the biblical story and to read the word that is spoken there. It is as if each of these different aspects of the biblical witness is pointing towards the same need that Archbishop Anthony Bloom discerned in the woman who came to consult him: the need to stop our frantic activity, discerning in stillness the word that God has been speaking to us all along.

Not only are many of the prayers we use in the course of Vespers examples of this process of shifting and shaping of experience to find the presence of God in the events that unfold, but so is the very process of praying the Divine Office, which involves repeated encounters with the same material over cyclical periods of liturgical season and calendar year. All of the Divine Office involves a gathering and chewing over of the biblical witness to God's activity. It can be seen as an extended lesson in how to approach the material of our own lives.

Occasionally, in the course of our journey, there will be rare experiences which arrive 'with the label attached'. These are the daybreak moments: what I earlier termed the 'soft places', where we might think we catch a glimpse of wings passing by. These 'light on' experiences, as the Carmelite prioress Ruth Burrows calls them, can be profoundly significant moments along our way. They are sometimes the crucial signposts that guide our journey. It nevertheless remains true that we, like Dante who found such a moment in his meeting with Beatrice, can revisit such times to great profit, uncovering ever new dimensions of the experience that did not disclose themselves to us at the time.

But for most of us, the majority of our experience will consist of that pattern of rough edges to which I referred in chapter three. The art of our days seems the art of collage rather than the smooth surface of an airbrushed image. Apparently shapeless events, or even tragic moments, but mostly just the monotony of a rather predictable and apparently featureless landscape. It is perhaps for this reason that we share Peer Gynt's concern about the core of the onion. It can be very difficult to answer the spiritual director's classic question, 'Where is God in this?', when we are not even sure where *we* are in this, never mind anybody else. Our temptation at such moments (and there are many of them) is to join the likes of Peer Gynt in a relentless forward movement – I will work hard, achieve, above all keep moving forward, to distract myself from the worry, the terror, that it all amounts to nothing.

Confusion will, as we all recognise, frequently be the shaggy staple of our daily tapestry, but there comes a moment later in the day when the elements of the tapestry begin to take shape. We are offered the chance to gaze more profoundly, to realise that perhaps we were simply looking at the tapestry from the wrong side. Now we can begin to notice the patterns that we have been weaving: but this is a pattern formed from the whole of who we are. Cutting away the layers, selective self-editing, will destroy the beauty of the weave. No sense will emerge.

Using this metaphor of the shaping of a life as the weaving of fabric, the Welsh poet Jean Earle, in her poem 'The Woollen Mill', invites us to

> Look back, from evening. A widespread day
> Maddened yet silked with light . . .

I suppose every turn of the earth
Is loom to someone's light.
A skein untangles
Out of wind and sun,
Lies in the ordered warp, patterning
Scarlet, blue –

The cross is taken. ³

A footnote to the poem informs us that 'taking the cross' is a defining stage in the weaving process. The coincidence of images is a happy one. As the story of Christ meets our personal story, as we 'take the cross', a coherent pattern emerges. It is the particular grace of the evening moment to offer us an awareness of 'a true pattern', as 'the cross is taken in the warp/ And the weave is certain'.

The office of Vespers invites us to engage with a process of reflection on the journey as the day moves towards evening. This is about looking back, learning from what has already been, the process of 'chewing over' experience and reshaping it in order to learn lessons only available from a later perspective; allowing the landscape to reshape itself from novel vistas. The evening light reveals new aspects of the day we had failed to see because we were too busy. We now encounter what the literary critic Christopher Ricks, writing of Milton's poetic technique, called 'tincture and reflection' – that is, the intricate patterning effect of one event, one relationship, one decision, upon another in the shape of our lives: the sense that emerges when these situations are seen together, rather than encountered separately as we hurry along our everyday way.

It is characteristic of the reflective attitude to life that it constantly discovers new depths in experiences we thought we had completely understood. I recently revisited a portion of my childhood by travelling to what used to be my grandparents' home – a Yorkshire town, where they lived in a typically suburban house with a small garden. Physically, little had changed in the neighbourhood, but as I walked among the memories, they emerged to tell me new stories. My later life reflected back onto the earlier events, a tincture of the present coloured the memories of days now gone. But I recognised themes in far-off events that would emerge again and again in more recent happenings. Present and past, apparently separated by such a distance of time, coloured one another and, as they met, new sense emerged. One of the most vital disciplines in the spiritual life is this process of touching the deepest parts of ourselves: allowing Christ to open the scroll and to 'explain the scriptures' to us. The traditional monastic route to this recollection of who we are is the process of slow, prayerful reading of the biblical story.

The *Rule for Monks* requires that the brethren devote a significant proportion of each day to a task the author terms 'holy reading', in Latin: *lectio divina*. I doubt whether any modern monastery allows the proportion of the day suggested by Benedict to this prayerful practice, which could be described as the characteristic monastic activity. It is one that can offer a way into addressing the question of owning and understanding our own experience.

Lectio divina can be seen as a cyclical pattern of chewing over of biblical experience, and in many respects it forms the underpinning of the whole monastic way of life. The monastic pattern of living, in repeated cycles, with great attention to everything, is actually the pattern for lectio divina.

One way to understand lectio is that it begins in a process of slow reading – the precise opposite of the 'speed reading' we hear so much about in the context of efficiency and time management. Where the speed reader is consciously skimming surfaces, the slow reader tries to engage with depth. Where there is an emphasis on outcomes in reading purposefully, the slow reader has no particular aim in mind – like the person who sets out for a country walk, we are travelling to admire the view, to enjoy the process of walking, not to arrive anywhere in particular. There is something immediately satisfying in standing a series of contemporary shibboleths on their heads.

One contemporary writer stumbled upon the practice of slow reading by sheer chance, as a result of having only one book

available to him when he was interned in a POW camp during the
Second World War. Sidney Piddington explains that he started
out with the simple object of making his book last, but that it
quickly dawned upon him that what he terms 'super-slow reading'
was a fruitful pursuit in its own right. Two weeks of slow
reading covered only ten pages. 'I spent three hours on two short
chapters,' he tells us, 'savouring each paragraph, lingering over a
sentence, a phrase, or even a single word.'[4] But in this process he
encountered a refreshment of spirit that was wholly unexpected.
He had discovered the dimension of depth in reading, and was
learning to allow himself to sink into the text:

> Sometimes just a particular phrase caught my attention,
> sometimes a sentence. I would read it slowly, analyse it,
> read it again – perhaps changing down into an even lower
> gear – and then sit for twenty minutes thinking about it
> before moving on.[5]

What Piddington is describing would be recognised immediately by monastics from all ages: this is a beginning to the listening
'with the ear of the heart' that Benedict calls for from his monks
as they read the scriptures or reflect on their experience. It is
intriguing to find secular seekers stumbling upon age-old
Christian practices, and finding them life-giving and supportive
(sometimes in extreme circumstances). At the same time it is
worrying to think that we have these treasures on offer, but have
succeeded in burying them where no one will find them – a little
like the 'unworthy servant' of the parable.

The process of lectio itself was never described by Benedict,
who appears to take it for granted that his reader already knows
what is involved. It seems quite likely that the distinction between
'slow reading' and what we would today call 'speed reading'
would never have occurred to him or his contemporaries. All
reading was slow. But the way Benedict writes is already an
illustration of lectio in practice. Like most ancient Christian
writers, he sews together scriptural sentences from widely scattered sources, interspersing them with his own insights, weaving
a texture that suggests an author who has mulled over this material

many times. The Word has entered the fabric of his thinking. In Jean Earle's phrase, 'The cross is taken in the warp/ And the weave is certain.'

Helpfully for us moderns, there are accounts of this form of prayer from monastic sources in later periods, and a living tradition of lectio within monastic communities. One written account that I find especially illuminating was penned by the twelfth-century Carthusian Prior Guigo. Guigo was one of the first – perhaps the very first – systematically to divide up the prayer of lectio into a series of four distinct stages, which he likens to the rungs of a ladder. Like most medievals, Guigo clearly loves to systematise, and we could be misled into thinking that his 'stages' are totally discrete events, or that a later one is somehow superior to an earlier. But provided we are not too literally-minded about his system, the pattern he proposes is helpful – at the very least as a way of beginning to understand the various moods and movements of the prayer form he is introducing. The four stages are described by Guigo in the following way:

> Reading is a directing of the mind to a careful looking at the scriptures. Meditation is a studious activity of the mind, probing the knowledge of some hidden truth under the guidance of our own reason. Prayer is a devout turning of the heart to God to get ills removed or to obtain good things. Contemplation is a certain elevation above itself of the mind which is suspended in God, tasting the joys of eternal sweetness.[6]

The prayer of slow reading begins with the choice of a short passage of scripture – it might, for example, be chosen from the liturgy of the day. The monastic offices are littered with gemstone paragraphs from Old and New Testaments, nuggets placed to promote the practice of lectio arising from the office itself. Simply and quietly, we read over the chosen verses, attending first to the literal meaning – formal scripture study isn't a prerequisite to lectio, but it can help to ground our prayer in the historical meaning of the text. The task here is neither to speculate nor to reflect, but simply to listen, to wait upon the Word. Repeated readings of the passage, pauses, silences are the natural shape of such a first stage.

Guigo tells us that 'Reading *looks for the sweetness* of the life of blessedness, meditation locates it, prayer asks for it, contemplation tastes it'; [7] so the purpose of the first step on the ladder of lectio is to allow a phrase or sometimes just a word to stand out from the passage, to echo into the chamber of the heart. It will be a 'sweetness' that tells us where to look – something will stand out for us, and it is with this phrase or sentence that we should then remain, allowing the rest of the passage to fall away. What are we drawn to, struck by, in the passage? This is the place to look.

There is no right length of time to spend on any step of the ladder, we might be relieved to hear. Lectio is not a 'system' for prayer – it is an invitation to encounter the word. So just as in any time of prayer, we should allow the spirit to move our hearts at his own pace. There's no hurry. Sometimes we may simply wish to sit with the passage as a whole, or to take a phrase and repeat it, almost like a mantra. 'Truly,' says the psalmist, 'I have set my soul in silence and peace. As a weaned child in its mother's arms, even so is my soul'. The image is apposite: we nurture and nurse the word as it works its mysterious magic within us. There is no need to think about it – a simple savouring of the sound may be what we are drawn to for quite some time. We may love a particular image, a picture in the mind, that the text creates. Alternatively, we may buzz with inspired thought about the text. All of these are fine.

When we are ready, we move to the 'meditation' stage of the prayer, taking the phrase or word that has settled in our heart and 'chewing' it – as Guigo memorably expresses it. The second rung of the ladder is a 'breaking of the word', opening up the brief scriptural phrase that has been turning around within us, beginning to engage actively where previously we have been simply receptive.

The monastic offices of the day are one of the contexts that model this process for us. Each psalm in the divine office is framed by an antiphon – a brief 'thought', sometimes drawn from the psalm text itself, and sometimes from another scriptural source which has parallels to the psalm that the choir has chanted. This antiphon is to the psalm as a whole as the mantra-phrase or sentence is to the passage we have been reading – it is the nugget that sums up the whole for us at this specific moment of reflection.

Monks of old would sometimes improvise these antiphons, as 'psalm prayers', arising from the psalm in the intervals between chanting, and this is what we are invited to do in the lectio process, chewing over the images or ideas that the scriptural nugget has begun to surface in our minds and hearts. As we move into the meditation we consciously turn to the mood we have entered, the images that are passing through our minds, the events of the recent or distant past that this passage of scripture has brought to us. Perhaps we are moved to question, to praise, to lament or simply to marvel. Perhaps we are confused and un-certain. The essence of the meditation is that we simply allow the text to resonate with the thoughts it has stirred in us, and notice what has begun to appear. A landscape within us has been called into being by this Word, the spirit is brooding, now we should allow the light to shine across that landscape and begin to explore it.

We may be moved to reflect actively upon why we have focused upon this specific passage, we may need to probe our reactions to a phrase we find difficult or worrying: why do we feel this way, why are these images coming to mind?

This is not formal Bible study, so it is not only possible but actually desirable that our encounter with the Word should call up awareness of dimensions of our own lives – memories, events from the recent or distant past, our concerns about friends, people we find difficult. As we do this, our story meets the story told in scripture, they mingle and something we may not have fully understood before, or not considered previously in this specific way can begin to emerge. 'The cross is taken'. This mutual interrogation of my own story and the story of the scriptures is a central experience in the prayer of slow reading.

Once again there is no absolutely right time for this to take, and no outcome as such that is sought. This prayer is just as valid if we find we are simply sitting in the presence of the Word as if we are moved to make a particular change in our lives. Sometimes a seed is planted at this moment of stillness, but it is for God to water the seed. In slow reading, by definition there is no hurry.

In one sense, a monk's whole life is an extended meditation, mixing the psalm texts with the life text, day after day, week after week, year after year – watching the fields to see what God will cause to grow. But a meditation can also be less leisurely and have a sense of progression if that is how it develops, and when we are ready we can move on to the stage Guigo specifically terms 'prayer', in which we articulate our emerging hopes, fears, aspirations and concerns as prayers to God, talking to him out of the issues that the meditation has generated in our hearts.

The moment of prayer on the third rung of Guigo's ladder is one of those mysteriously lovely moments in which the miracle of grace at work in us is sometimes almost tangible. The scriptural word, which we receive in faith as the Word who is Christ, provokes in us a surfacing of the issues we face in this particular moment of our lives, and, as it mixes with those issues, it inspires in us further words of faith, of praise or of petition – Christ prays in us, the Word is made flesh, and we become as 'Other Christs', syllables of the great prayer to the Father that is the very being of the Son in eternity. 'Heaven in ordinary', as the poet George Herbert puts it.[8]

According to Guigo, 'Reading, as it were, puts the solid food into our mouths, meditation chews it and breaks it down, prayer obtains the flavour of it, and contemplation is the very sweetness which makes us glad and refreshes us'.[9] Contemplation, in which we move into a silence that lovingly attends upon God, is the final rung of Guigo's ladder. When there are no more words, the heart waits quietly in the presence of the unseen God. The moment of contemplation is classically described in the medieval English text *The Cloud of Unknowing* as 'a naked intent towards God, the desire for him alone', and in many medieval sermons as 'the soul's Sabbath day rest'.[10] It may be either purposeful silence or restful refreshment, and it may last but a moment or it may be a stillness in which we persist for a substantial period of our prayer time. This is a deliberately contrary exercise – a willing wasting of time with God. Nothing happens. That is the whole point.

Implicit in Guigo's use of the ladder image is the typical perspective of medieval churchmen, that contemplation is the highest form of the Christian life – so the ladder can make the prayer of slow reading seem simply a preparation for silence before God. It can be used in this way, of course, and it is perfectly valid to do so: but in practice, this can lead to an impoverishment of the other movements within the lectio. The monk and lectio have been frequently likened to the cow chewing the cud – the stages are iterative. Like so many aspects of the Benedictine life, repetition is of the essence. We store up something from one step of the ladder, returning to it later – chewing afresh, as it were. Sometimes when we use this prayer, the lectio stage itself – reading – is all we may need or want. On other occasions we will slip very naturally and appropriately up and down Guigo's ladder, reading, meditating, praying, and then repeating the sequence. There is no reason why the steps have to be in this order on all occasions. The prayer of slow reading is intended to be very flexible.

The feeding metaphor which runs through Guigo's account of the prayer of lectio is a widely-used image to describe this form of prayerfully nourishing the soul with the Word. It helps, by its very physical, sensuous quality, to overcome any initial inclination we might have to suppose that this prayer is a wholly cerebral, thinking exercise. Lectio is clearly intended to engage the whole of our energies with the encounter with God in his Word. The Russian Orthodox classic *The Way of The Pilgrim*, which introduced many Westerners to the Jesus Prayer, touches on the same point when the pilgrim discovers that the prayer phrase he has been repeating, the mantra-like 'Lord Jesus, have mercy on me, a sinner', has taken up an almost physical lodging in his heart. It seems that the prayer is repeating itself there, accompanying the breathing of his lungs and the beating of his heart. The phrase we are using in lectio may sometimes 'lodge' in the same way, staying with us for extended periods of time. The Word can become flesh, lodging in our hearts: and the Word that has lodged in our heart prays us.

The monastic life, cyclically patterned around daily, weekly, seasonal and annual encounters with the mysteries of Christ in the scriptures and the actions of the liturgy is a patterning of life as lectio. As we weave our days around our lectio, 'the cross is taken in the warp/ And the weave is certain'. This is a true route to making the divine narrative, God's story, into our story – it is the long and arduous task of bringing our lives into God's light. It is significant that this prayerful reading is a slow process, and that it relies upon repetition. The emergence of coherence is never rapid. We need to allow sense to manifest itself at its own speed and in its own ways.

The prayer of slow reading provides a model for how we might bring elements of our own personal stories into our prayerful chewing. Just as the Bible contains the sacred stories of our faith community, which we encounter in the liturgy and in our own prayerful reading, even so each of us has a personal canon of the sacred stories of our lives. These are the stories we tell our-selves about who we are, where we have come from and what our journey means to us. These stories are the ways we explore the landscapes of our lives. We can use several techniques to reconnect ourselves with these stories.

One of the great travellers of the last century was the writer Bruce Chatwin. In his novel *The Songlines* he writes about his encounter with the culture of the native people of Australia. This culture, which the aboriginals succeeded in hiding from the white settlers for many generations, has a remarkable lesson for us in the task of reclaiming the landscape of our life.

According to Chatwin, the key to understanding the aboriginal outlook is the vivid awareness in that culture of the capacity of a place to be a repository of the scared memory of the tribe. The ancestors, mythic figures of the dreamtime, are thought of as having traversed the country before the age of humanity began.

As they journeyed, the ancestors sung into being each feature of the Australian landscape, incorporating their own stories into rocks, rivers and high hills. For a native Australian, the landscape sings the songs of the ancestors. The story they told of them-selves – the story that brought the natural world into being – is waiting in the landscape, if one learns how to read it aright.

Chatwin tells us that 'the whole of Australia could be read as a musical score. There was hardly a rock or a creek in the country that could not or had not been sung. One should perhaps visualise the *Songlines* as a spaghetti of *Iliads* and *Odysseys*, writhing this way and that, in which every "episode" was readable in terms of geology.'[11]

This is a profound and moving approach to the landscape – when I know the songs of the ancestors, each element of the natural world takes on a transparency to depth. Each is a marker on the journey of my own people to arrive at where we now are. The landscape is biography presented in terms of geology. As the artist Luke Elwes puts it: 'The lines are the paths of our own life, and the meandering course of all life, of branches, trees, roots and riverbeds. In their uninterrupted movement lies the search for markers, the signposts we need if we are to draw our own maps.'[12]

Our western European culture has not offered us a way of understanding the landscape of our lives with the same coherence as the profound and poetic approach of the native Australians. Compared to the aboriginals, with their far-reaching sense of their own rootedness in the landscape, it is we settled people who appear the homeless nomads. Our concern throughout this book has been to locate the action of God in the events and experiences of our lives, and to be more consciously aware of how we might identify and reclaim this landscape. Chatwin's account of the Songlines allows us to look into different aspects of the world and find that we better understand the face we see reflected back to us. We can try to look at both the physical and the psychological landscapes of our own lives in more depth and learn our own songs. The image of the Songlines offers a way into reclaiming the material we leave scattered around.

The gospel parable of the shepherd who loses one of his hundred sheep makes clear the value that God places upon each one of us. We can each be rather more profligate with our own lives – we leave bits of them lying around, and do not always trouble to pick them up again. God goes in search of the stray: we tend to hope someone will brush it under the carpet. At the same time, we dig in to defend the attenuated version of ourselves in a way that makes the achievement of wholeness even less likely. The lectio process, a slow circling about and chewing over of material that we do not pretend to exhaust in one session, is a valuable model for how we might approach the reclaiming of aspects of ourselves. By prayerfully reflecting upon our own lives we can allow the pattern we have woven over the years to begin to emerge in its true colours. As has so often been true in our journey, this is a process of encountering depth, not surface, and can only happen slowly.

A visit to a small market town on the Welsh border provided me with an insight into the process of touching my own story. Stepping into Hay-on-Wye was akin to a trip into the lumber room of my mind. I am one of those people who – soon after the age of five, when (I am told) I declared that I did not want to learn to read – began reading, found that I loved it, and never gave up. Most of my life has been accompanied by books. Hay is a book-lover's paradise: its narrow streets rejoice in some thirty or forty bookshops – antiquarian books tumble into murder mystery, the occult rubs shoulders with children's classics. Nothing, it seems, that we have committed to paper has failed to find a place in one or more of its gloriously eccentric shelves.

I spent a fascinating afternoon browsing these rich pastures. In every bookshop I entered I met many old favourites: books I had read, editions I once owned, books I remembered wanting to read but not getting around to – each of them linked to significant moments in my life. Experiences I had not thought about for years, feelings that I forgotten, encounters, friendships, losses – each shop, each shelf, opened up forgotten moments of child-hood, youth and my adult years.

This walk around the bookstacks of Hay-on-Wye was almost

literally a trip down memory lane. It was as if significant sections of my own life had taken on physical substance as a town, and I had been given the privilege of walking its streets. This is precisely the undertaking to which we are invited – to reclaim the key moments, the highways and byways, the journey as it has unfolded for us.

A walk in the country is a refreshment for the spirit, as we are all aware. But there are places that we find especially powerful because of the events that took place there. Usually these will be personal memories, but I have certainly known places that touch something I had not known I was aware of.

Each morning, I have the joy of walking a hundred yards from the monastery to my office in the boarding-house I supervise. I call it a joy because the walk takes me along a terrace overlooking one of the finest views in Sussex – a wooded valley stretches before me, descending in the distance towards fields, with farms glimpsed towards the horizon. I think of this walk as a crucial lung breathing fresh air into the busy day that lies ahead. This is a significant place for me: not simply a place of great beauty, but a landscape redolent with memories. Can I read a land-scape, finding the phrases that address me and reflecting upon them?

The valley, with its woods and fields, is littered with memories, if I walk slowly along its paths and pause in hollows and beneath trees. Here I first walked when I was a newcomer. This was the path I took one day when lost, and only the sound of distant bells told me the way back. Along this track a conversation took place that changed the way I thought about an issue that concerned me.

Each of us can use the physical landscape that surrounds us to touch memories associated with particular places. To revisit the place where a significant event took place is to step back into that moment, allowing something within us to energise our sense of ourselves, to challenge us – perhaps to distress us, and to give us pause. Memory is a puzzle – sometimes we need the physical presence of a place before we can enter completely into memories which are active all the time but only to be grasped when we stand within the location they are caught up with. The memory may delight or disturb, but when we step back into the place we allow the story to be told, the song to be sung.

The native Australians think of the singing of the memories as the way the world is held in being. To sing the ancestors' songs is to remake and sustain the world. We are very shy of such notions, preferring to think of the world as merely a self-sustaining physical engine, held together by the objective laws of physics and chemistry, moving to the music of mathematics. But whether this is true of the physical world or not, it certainly is not true of the lived world we inhabit, made up of personal encounters and opening constantly into profound psychological depth and transcendent spiritual height. Of this world, this place we have 'really been', the aboriginal insight holds true. If we fail to sing this landscape it will not be sustained in health and vitality.

We can sing the stories of our well-loved gardens, just as Isaiah sang the song of his vineyard, discovering our childhood memories; or perhaps the precious moments of bringing up our own children. We can reflect on the physical places we find significant – prayerful walks through the garden, or the area in which we live. It may be that our neighbourhood is unattractive, but that does not prevent it being rich with images and memories. Some of these may have the sinewy power of anger, or the colour of dismay. Instead of hurrying past, from time to time we should step into the images these places open up in our minds.

A friend always prays on the seashore. There is a weight of powerful memory for him tied up in a particular seafront kiosk. Another friend has a 'safe place' she goes to in the woods when times are difficult. I wonder what the experience of arriving there might be like, as the place extends its welcome to the troubled spirit? A third person I know loves to walk the city streets, finding that the combination of company and aloneness that the street provides is perfect for prayer, while the people and buildings she passes evoke every conceivable human strength and weakness – every glory and every frailty.

Some of the most tragic of human conflicts are associated with the sense of memory caught up in place. The Holy Places in Israel are a clear case in point.

But our personal 'holy places' need not become the occasion of conflict – rather, they can be a solace and bring healing. Even if the memories associated with some places are difficult, they remain important and must be honoured.

Our homes, for example, can be prayed in the same way – the walls of our houses, and the very stones of the garden may be reservoirs of memories which we need to touch from time to time if we are to see the shape of where we have been and where we are going.

Many of us only find the opportunity to sort through the archives of our past in this way when a parent dies and the task of sorting out what had been a much-loved family home falls upon those who are left behind. There is wisdom in treading these paths in less traumatic times, for while I have known friends who found the experience of clearing up the house was therapeutic, a part of the grieving and healing process, I think I have known more people for whom it was itself a part – a significant part – of the pain of losing a loved one.

We can pray these places rather in the same manner as lectio, described earlier. Why is the place important? What has it touched in us? Sometimes the answer is obvious, but at other times we may discover surprises, and uncover dimensions we had neglected or simply forgotten. Prayer can arise from this consideration, just as it did from the scriptures we considered before.

But the landscape of life, the singing of memories, can be entered not only through the literal, physical landscape around us, but also via a series of paths that are waiting for us to notice them and begin our journey. Once again, they are the stuff of our everyday, and so we may not always honour them by recognising in them a series of doors to the sacred.

One method that may suit people who have lived busy family lives is to pray through the family photo album. I know many people who have maintained a vital and lively record of the people, places and events of their lives through photos. One of my own community has maintained an enviable record of every development that has ever occurred in the buildings the community inhabits – although he has a tendency to miss out the people; another monk has a superb collection of photos he took while involved in missionary work in rural Peru. I am sure that both the glorious countryside of the Rio Apurimac and the smiling faces of those to whom he ministered contain a wealth of sacred stories for him.

A family I know well has covered almost every inch of wall space in the family home with a visual record of their children growing up. Walking through their home is a joy, even for the casual visitor. They have created an associative house, every part of which opens into memories of significant moments in their life as a family. I found myself pausing to share a party, a first day at school, a family ski trip. The experience stays with me as a remarkable privilege – for a short time I was allowed to share someone else's songs, to know their sacred stories and to tread a landscape that was not my own but where I knew I was welcome.

When the photographs are our own, it is a rewarding and revealing exercise to sit quietly with a collection of photographs, letting each image speak its particular story to us. What memories does it open up? What contexts does it bring to mind? If it is a photo of someone who has played a major role in our lives, this can be a moment for quiet thanksgiving, or perhaps for a prayer that memories may be healed. There may be invitations to reconciliation or a call to rethink the way we behave.

Some of us will have kept diaries, and some may have – at least from some periods of our lives – complete journals. Letters are another source of excellent paths into prayer. Sometimes, the physical material of which these documents are made resonates with memory.

The images – paintings or other art work – with which we decorate our homes or which we see regularly in public places, can open doors into material we need to deal with. In my community, we used to hang an image of the Last Supper in a prominent place in a community room. This image is a relief sculpture from Peru, the work of an outstanding South American artist. It was a gift to monks of this community who had been working among the poor in Lima, the capital of Peru. The figures in the sculpture are clearly Peruvians with their work-roughened hands and distinctly native facial features. In the warm ochres and browns of the clay, they are caught in various postures of agony and strife. Unlike many Last Supper scenes, this is an image of the disciples as men who are torn by disagreement. The moment the artist has chosen to portray is the moment of Judas' betrayal, and – at the centre of the group – Christ's arms are spread wide, as if to 'take the cross'. The image is powerful. It is full of the force of a group of men disagreeing. It contains the tragedy of a continent, but it speaks the intimate language of human relationships: most particularly, relationships between men.

Many of the community hated the sculpture, but it is ironic to reflect that it was only when we took the painful decision that our manpower no longer allowed us to maintain a presence in Latin America that this image was put away in a cupboard.

A community of men living and working together is not always an easy place to be. Idealism and religious devotion, good things in themselves, do not automatically produce soft edges. Interactions can be demanding and problematic. Like the figures in the sculpture, we can find ourselves in real conflicts. But I am not surprised that we are sometimes inclined to hide this fact from ourselves, preferring to project an image of calm and mutual friendliness, or a very English sort of politeness. We need to be very honest when we disagree, but for the most part we do not do this. We often paper over the cracks.

It saddened and disturbed me that my own community were unable to see that we were the men depicted in that Last Supper sculpture. At the very moment when the image of Christ's Last Supper depicted our reality, we were unprepared to allow this potent symbol of our situation to lead us deeper into our own grieving. A sad moment, but not really a surprising one. It is a rare person who can gaze steadily at grief, and communities have similar reactions. We had to move more slowly: the sculpture was too steep a slope for us to ascend. Perhaps one day we will be ready to look at it again, and able to deal with the difficult message it contains.

From time to time in this book I have used moments from films to illuminate or to explore aspects of my own experience. This is a practice that seems obvious, once one encounters it, but I would have to acknowledge having treated film as 'mere entertainment' for quite a long time. We are not given much encouragement to use the mass media for the development of our personal spirituality – sadly, the primary attitude religious people are perceived as having towards the media is one of criticism, and constant calls for censorship.

My own attitude to film was challenged and changed by an encounter with a remarkable man, a psychotherapist by profession, who has made a significant discovery about the way in which the recollection of filmic moments can assist us in bringing to the surface some of the messages our minds are speaking to us, but which we haven't taken the trouble to hear.

Bernie Wooder invites his clients to recall moments from films they have seen which have really stood out for them. He then works with them to discover what it was about that particular moment that has been significant for the client. Bernie tells of a client 'who would always break down in "The Colour Purple" – not a film I would have expected him to feel emotionally close to. The scene which always got to him was the one in which the Whoopi Goldberg character is being sung to. He said that what made him cry was that she was being focused on not for anything she'd won or achieved but because she was her. Through that, we were able to talk about his own family background where people were viewed in the light of their achievements – and his own self image as an adult.'[13] Another example was the Christmas favourite 'It's A Wonderful Life', which allows many people who have made sacrifices throughout their lives to face and begin to address the anger that they often feel, but which they have never been able to articulate.

Ancient Indian peoples in the Americas practised a tradition known today as 'the Vision Quest'. In a similar way to the ancient European practice of 'incubating' a dream which was regarded as containing a message from the gods, the young person who is setting out in life 'seeks his fortune' by seeking out a dream, a vision, from which the symbols will be guides for the path ahead. This way of thinking through the images from films could have parallels to such a tradition of significant imagery.

Dreams themselves can certainly be modes of divine revelation. The Bible is full of dreams and bursting with dreamers. Old and New Testaments identify the 'visions of the night' as a primary vehicle whereby God speaks in the lives of those who seek to know his will. Jacob sees a vision of the ladder linking earth and heaven, Joseph is a dreamer and an interpreter of dreams, Daniel is a seer who can perceive the truth of dreams. In Matthew's gospel, especially, dreams are powerful signs from God to Joseph and to the wise men who seek the infant Jesus. Our lack of interest in our dreaming in the modern church is a sad indicator of the want of imagination that afflicts many dimensions of church life and can threaten to dry up the spirit. We should be trying to search out what the poet Francis Thompson termed 'the traffic of Jacob's ladder/ Pitched betwixt Heaven and Charing Cross.'[14]

When we spend time reading slowly through our lives in any of these ways we are beginning to identify the action of God in our everyday. We begin to unify, to find coherence where there had been chaos. By bringing the life-stuff we encounter here into the *lectio* of scripture we vivify the dialogue between our personal story and the story God is telling, and the one illuminates the other.

As is often true, a story from the Egyptian Desert Fathers can provide a helpful way of understanding the role of this reclaiming within the whole of our spiritual lives.

Three brothers, we are told, set out on their life's path. One wanted to serve the poor, and devoted himself to their welfare in a busy city. The second was aflame with the message of the gospel, and wanted to preach to the heathen. He travelled to far-off lands to spread the word. Their youngest brother chose to go into the desert, inspired by the heroic tales that were told of the monks and their battles with the demons. He became a monk among the hermits of Scete.

CROSSING

Some years later, the two older brothers returned from their
labours, tired and disillusioned. No matter how hard the first
brother worked, and no matter how many people he helped,
there were always more poor people whom he was unable to
help. The second had a similar tale to tell: although he had planted
the gospel among untold thousands, there were many more who
had refused to listen, and a still larger number whom he had
never even reached. Both were troubled in their hearts, turbulent
dissatisfaction allowed them no peace.

Their hermit brother led them to a desert oasis, and stirred
the water of the pool with his staff.

'What do you see?' he asked each of them in turn, inviting
them to gaze into the moving water. The answer, of course, was
that neither brother could see anything except the water itself as
the ripples disturbed the surface.

'And so it is in your distracted, turbulent lives. There is no
calm, no stillness in you – and so there is no peace in your work,
no presence of God in your mission for the gospel.'

The hermit waited until the water was calm and repeated his
question. This time the brothers saw not only their own faces
clearly reflected in the still pool, but also the trees of the oasis,
the blue of the heavens, and the figures of their companions
standing beside them. It was hardly necessary for their brother to
point the moral of the story. Needless to say, the two older
brothers joined him in the hermit life of the desert.

The story, as most commentators point out, is a fairly blatant
piece of monastic propaganda, stressing the superiority of the
monastic path to any other response to the gospel. But its value
lies in the fact that neither the struggle for social justice nor the
task of preaching the gospel can be undertaken as an escape from
the truth about ourselves. If this is what happens, then however
much good we may do, we are involved in something less than a
Christian life.

The desert story points to a very simple but vital reality: the
place where we will find the action of God is in the details of our
own lives, as we reflect upon the story he is telling in us. Our
personal story needs to be brought constantly into the context of

the greater story that is the scriptural Word of God, but there is no substitute for bringing our whole selves into this context. An attenuated humanity, a set of fragments will not do. The glory of God, as Iranaeus famously puts it, is a fully alive human being. We can only be fully alive when we allow the whole of our own story to come together, when we reclaim the landscape of our life.

5
Walking Away
Compline (Night Prayer)

That hesitant figure, eddying away
Like a winged seed loosened from its parent stem,
Has something I never quite grasp to convey
About nature's give-and-take — the small, the scorching
Ordeals which fire one's irresolute clay.

I have had worse partings, but none that so
Gnaws at my mind still. Perhaps it is roughly
Saying what God alone could perfectly show —
How selfhood begins with a walking away,
And love is proved in the letting go.
                    C. Day Lewis, 'Walking Away'[1]

IN THE MONASTERY the day ends as it began, in the darkness.
By the light of candles, the night office of Compline is chanted,
and the daily mystery of surrender becomes the monk's practice.
'Into your hands, Lord, I commend my spirit', we sing, echoing
the words of Christ on the cross. This is a prayer of dispossession,
a letting go of the striving and struggling that makes up so great a
proportion of our day. The practice of letting go might be taken
to be a soft-edged spiritual relaxation were it not for the original
context of those words from the cross. They establish the night
office as a reminder of the mystery of death that awaits us all.

We have now crossed the full course of the day. The evening, a
time of gathering insight and knowledge, now gives way to night

once more. The light fades and travelling must cease. Perhaps this movement back into the dark may seem to make a nonsense of all our map making, to tell us that exploring is futile. But we take with us into the darkness everything we have learned along the way, and the greatest lesson of all is found as we step once more into the night.

Only here, as the journey nears its end, can we recognise the fact that there is no pre-ordained path:

> Traveller, your footsteps are
> the path and nothing else.
> Traveller, there is no path;
> you make the path by walking. [2]

as the Spanish poet Antonio Muchado puts it. Everything that has happened to us along the way points to this one crucial realisation: how everything has been different from what we expected as we set out.

We want to be able to predict how things will be and then to gather up completed achievements, ticking off the items on our list. We then expect the varied dimensions of our lives to stay put. But, of course, they do not. Everything changes. We have convinced ourselves that only in an unchanging stability, a refuge from the storm of life, can we find happiness. But the reverse is true. If we insist that happiness derives from the unchanging, this very insistence will make us miserable. Wisdom lies in recognising what Brother Roger of Taizé has memorably called 'the dynamic of the provisional', the fact that is staring us in the face: we must let go of our desire to cling to what has been. We are always walking away. By so doing, we create the path.

Our only stability is that of fidelity to the journey itself, travelling forward on a way that is ever new and never fixed. Varying the metaphor, Muchado writes: 'Mankind owns four things that are no good at sea: rudder, anchor, oars, and the fear of going down.'[3] Were we wasting our time in mapping and exploring, then? No, because as every experienced teacher knows, although the finest lessons are those that arise spontaneously, this very spontaneity is the product of good planning. The art of improvisation, the dynamic of the provisional, does not consist in having no plan, but in knowing when the time has come to put the plan aside and walk away from what appeared to be the road.

A friend of mine is one of those people who suffers the misfortune of being dogged by minor disasters at every turn. Yet he is a meticulous planner, and frequently faces the indignity of watching the causal success of those far less well prepared than he is. He has still to learn that his problems usually arise as a direct consequence of his failure to let go, to tear up the plan at the crucial moment.

I have often found insights to assist my own journey by looking outside the Western traditions of faith, allowing the new perspective of the east to open up approaches I had not previously considered. Perhaps nowhere is the practice I have called letting go of the plan so directly addressed as in the Zen teachings of Japanese Buddhism. The 'koan', the contra-logical paradox in a saying or a story that teases and tantalises us, until it shatters the walls of our illusions, is a Zen practice from which the more prosaic argument of the West can profitably learn.

For many years I was puzzled by one of the most baffling of Zen Buddhism's many paradoxical sayings: 'If you meet the Buddha on the road, kill him'. To my uninformed Western outlook, the Zen paradox appeared impious at the very least. To slay the guide and teacher made no sense at all.

I suppose that as I pondered on the Zen saying, at the back of my mind was the Emmaus story in St Luke's gospel (Luke 24). In this story also, we find ourselves on the road, and encountering the guide and teacher. Luke tells us that two otherwise unknown followers of Jesus, Cleopas and his companion, are fleeing from Jerusalem. They are depressed and confused by the death of Jesus on Calvary, but as they walk along they meet the Risen Christ on the road — although, as is often the case in stories of the resurrection, they do not recognise him for who he is.

But they speak to the stranger, who asks them why they are so downcast. They listen to what he has to tell them, are consoled, and offer him hospitality. This seemed to me a more appropriate response than that suggested by the Zen saying. Why should they 'kill him'? What could the Eastern tradition have been advising?

Ultimately, it was by reflecting on the same gospel story that I found a way into the Zen paradox. The crucial point is that Cleopas and his friend believe they have already 'met' Christ: 'our hope had been that he was the one to set Israel free'. In other words, they have him categorised – he is 'Messiah'. As such, he is fitted into their world-view: he is the warrior king who will cast off the Roman yoke. But to approach Christ in this way is to suppose that he can be tamed, understood in categories which suit our purposes. And, as C. S. Lewis famously pointed out through the figure of the great lion, Aslan, in his Narnia tales, 'tame' is not an adjective one should consider applying to Christ.

In the Emmaus story, it is Christ himself who shows us what it means to 'kill the Buddha on the road': in response to Cleopas' inadequate account of who Jesus was and what his death meant, the stranger speaks words that 'kill' everything the disciples had thought they understood. 'You foolish men, so slow to understand . . .' This is the shattering of a blindness, the destruction of a false perspective. The disciples' hearts burn, their eyes are opened: 'they recognised him in the breaking of the bread', but once again, Christ is moving away from what they thought they had understood: 'he vanished from their sight'.

On the Emmaus road, Cleopas and his companion learn to 'kill the Buddha on the road'. They are freed from the dead Jesus they had made in their own image, by the astonishing and completely unexpected presence of the living Christ. Every time we might suppose that we have tamed God or domesticated the gospel (and most of us do this all the time) we must be prepared to 'kill the Buddha', to let go and walk away into a darkness that surprises us. The growth in wisdom which monastic life, like any spiritual path, is supposed to create should set us free to change and be changed. Stasis creates fossils, but only the dynamism of love creates human beings. It is the lesson of letting go that makes this most clear.

Letting go a little has become something of a fashion today:

everything from undertaking the latest celebrity diet to the environmentally-aware 'detox' programmes we find in Sunday magazines. We are told it is a good thing to dispossess ourselves of addictions and dependencies, which it surely must be. But we like to keep this process of 'giving up' on the fringes of life. Like most fads in the field of recreational spirituality, if we find it is beginning to cut into the more fundamental parts of our lives we start to worry.

To let go of something that is crucial to us, rather than a fringe detail, is frightening. We find that we are moving beyond the narrowly defined comfort zone we usually inhabit, and begin to panic. Like the novice swimmer who finds that he has strayed out of his depth, we will usually thrash desperately back to the side of the pool. Perhaps the clearest symbol of our lack of realism in this area is our failure to engage seriously with the reality of the process of dying and the fact of death. Like the film-maker and comedian Woody Allen our entire culture appears to be saying: 'I'm not frightened of dying, I just don't want to be there when it happens'. We ignore the reality of death, giving the impression that we suppose it to be something that only concerns other people, not ourselves.

In stark contrast to our everyday culture that anaesthetises us against the fear of death stands the perspective to be found in the monastic tradition. St Benedict admonishes his monks to 'keep death daily before your eyes' (RB4), and monasteries are places where the presence of death as a dimension of the journey of life is taken seriously. In this, we have something in common with Eastern cultures in general, and are at odds with the post-enlightenment West. The perspective adopted in the monastic context is well expressed by the Indian mystical poet Kabir: 'If you don't break your ropes while you are alive, do you think ghosts will do it for you after you are dead? The idea that the soul will join with the ecstatic just because the body is rotten is all fantasy. What is found now is found then. If you find nothing now you will simply end up with an empty apartment in the City of Death'. [4]

For Kabir, as for St Benedict, there is an urgency to the fact of death which we ignore at our peril. Because we do not remember death, we can actually forget to live. The task of 'breaking our ropes' as Kabir puts it, of letting go of what is holding us back and learning to walk away, these are life processes. They have to be worked through in the simple human interactions that make up our days, they will not be magically accomplished for us by a benevolent supernatural power in an anticipated hereafter. When we neglect this undertaking it is almost as though we supposed the entire process of living to be a dress rehearsal. We live as though there will always be one more chance, and next time we will get it right. But unlike James Bond, we only live once, and death reminds us that this is no dress rehearsal: this is the real thing. Either we do it now, or we will never do it at all.

But Woody Allen is, as usual, spot on in his diagnosis: we are terrified of what death involves, and really would much rather not have to think about it. At one point in the funeral service of a priest in the Greek church the language of the liturgy deals frankly with the fear we all experience about the great unknown. 'Why these bitter words of the dying, O brethren, which they utter as they go hence? I am parted from my brethren. All my friends do I abandon, and go hence. But whither I go, that understand I not, neither what shall become of me yonder; only God who hath summoned me knoweth.'[5] But these are words we find hard to hear. We prefer not to think about the experience of dying, and keep the fact of death as far from us as we can. It is too harsh a reality. Sometimes, religious contexts can be some of the hardest in which to deal frankly with death, because beliefs in the afterlife can be used, quite improperly, to shield us from the stark facts stated in the Greek prayer. It is sobering to reflect that the recent movement towards secular funeral liturgies has sometimes given rise to more powerful and more honest reflection on the ambiguity of our feelings about the fact of death than the funeral services of the mainstream churches.

It can often take exposure to another culture, or to the views of someone who is himself a member of another culture, to draw our attention to the fact that our negligent attitude to death is anything but natural and universal. In *The Tibetan Book of Living and Dying* Sogyal Rinpoche, a Buddhist monk and spiritual teacher, identifies this state of denial as one of the deepest malaises of modern western culture.

> When I first came to the West I was shocked by the contrast between the attitudes to death I had been brought up with, and those I now found . . . I learned that people today are taught to deny death and taught that it means nothing but annihilation and loss . . . Others look on death with a naïve, thoughtless cheerfulness, thinking that for some unknown reason death will work out all right for them, and that it is nothing to worry about.'[6]

He suggests that our contemporary obsession with youth, sex and power may have a connection to our parallel failure to honour old age, the disabled or those who lack status and that all of these issues may be traced back to the fearful denial of death that he finds endemic in Western culture.

The Western monastic tradition, like that of Tibet in which Sogyal Rinpoche was trained, encourages us to 'keep death daily before our eyes' (RB4). There is a way of misunderstanding this injunction that could turn it into a neo-gothic fascination with the macabre, but St Benedict was not a Victorian romantic. He would have found it easier to understand Dr Johnson's famous quip that the news of imminent death 'concentrates the mind wonderfully', because it was this concern with waking us up to the realities of how we live now that lay behind his concern with our awareness of death.

One monk headmaster is reputed to have disconcerted a gathering of the great and the good by boldly announcing that his school prepared its students not for Oxbridge, the City or the Guards, but for death. Although this can seem a bizarre claim, it is in fact a statement about how we prepare ourselves and our children for living. The Christian perspective is that only the person who tries to face the reality of death is able to approach the fullness of life.

Each monastery enters into death every night, as the night prayer candles are extinguished, the community disperse to their rooms, and the 'Summum Silencium', the great silence, falls over the house. I sometimes think of the individuals who make up this community to which I belong gathered by night, the living each in his individual room, the dead in the beautiful graveyard alongside the monastery building. I am very conscious of living within a tradition which not only extends back over centuries and crosses continents, but which above all exists between the living and the dead members of this one monastery. This pattern of life, which must have existed in many ancient societies, is found in very few contexts in the modern world. This is a great loss.

The memorials, graves, and sacred places of my own natural family are scattered across a wide area of the country. Most of them are in places that had no context within the lives of those who are buried there. I have visited very few of them, except on the occasion of the funeral. I find this a sad diminishment.

But a monastic family lives alongside its dead. Every individual in our small, hedged graveyard frequently walked the grass beneath which he now lies, and sat many times in the shade of the trees which now guard his grave. Those of us who come after can visit the monastery graveyard and find a gathering of friends, a lesson in perseverance or a witness to the values we have promised to live by. It is a wonderful thing to see the communion of saints so directly figured forth.

A monastic funeral is a particularly moving event. The coffin with the body of the dead monk is received in the Abbey Church on the night before he is to be buried, and he joins the community in choir one last time. Throughout the night, candles burn beside the coffin, and the brethren visit informally to pray and to say their goodbyes. The funeral liturgy takes place in the church where the monk lived and worshipped, and his coffin makes its final journey to the graveyard in the monastery garden borne by the brethren who have lived alongside him. It is deeply moving to lower the coffin of a friend and brother into the earth beside others with whom we have all spent happy times.

But St Benedict is not simply concerned that we should honour the dead of our communities and families, but most especially that our outlook should be suffused with the awareness that our own death is a reality. Such a 'momento mori', a constant remembering of death, is so alien to the culture we inhabit that however hard we try we inevitably perceive something negative or even morbid in the perspective being suggested. How can this final lesson of the monk's day be the life-giving Word of the gospel for us?

The poet Cecil Day Lewis, writing of his experience as a parent of 'walking away' from his son on the boy's first day at school, points out that:

> . . . selfhood begins with a walking away,
> And love is proved in the letting go.

If we explore this 'walking away', which I suggest is exactly what Kabir meant by 'cutting knots', we may begin to find the good news in the process of letting go. We will discover that a cultural myth of our society, closely linked to our denial of death, is that the more tightly I hold onto the other people in my life, the more I love them. Sadly, the reverse is the case, but so insidiously widespread is the common view that we can very easily adopt it without question.

As a celibate monk, I have no family or children of my own, but for several years I worked as a housemaster in the boarding school attached to the monastery. In boarding pastoral care there are experiences which, to some extent, parallel those of a parent.

The pastoral staff of a boarding school become involved with their students as an extended family. Sorrows and joys are shared; like a parent one has the great privilege of playing a role in the process whereby a child becomes an adult. This is sometimes a tortuous and traumatic journey, but also a joyous and heady achievement for both students and staff. A young person whose life touches one's own for a period of years can become a significant part of the pastoral carer's life. But there comes a moment when the time has come to say goodbye – because the teacher's role is not like that of the parent, and the teacher only accompanies for a part of the journey.

I heave a hearty sigh of relief as each school year ends. Once the school holidays have eased the exhaustion that all teachers know only too well, however, I miss the daily involvement in the small and large details of the lives of the young people I work with. There is a strange dislocation involved in moving from a quasi-family of sixty to quasi-bachelorhood, especially when the process takes place overnight. Perhaps in some small way this annual process of becoming marginal gives me an insight into the experience of a parent as the family grows up.

I am sure that any parent of grown-up children who is reading these words will recognise the mixture of pride and sorrow with which one watches the fledglings leave the nest. Sometimes the desire to continue nurturing and protecting is almost over-whelming: but our greatest gift to our newly-adult children, whether we are parents or teachers, is to respect their autonomy, and by believing in them sufficiently to let go of them, to give them the space and the courage to discover who they are. Watching someone you love make a mistake is infinitely worse than making one's own errors, and I have no doubt that a parent's heart is broken many times in this process. I have felt the dimmest shadow of this pain in my role as a teacher. But this is a crucial lesson. The parent's letting go of her children is perhaps the greatest practice in dispossession it is possible to encounter. If we can let go here, perhaps we shall be free and perhaps our children shall be free.

'The culmination of our loving will be dispossession. Those whom we love, we must let go; we must let them be. Does my love for another give them freedom to make their own lives and leave me free?'[7] asks Timothy Radcliffe, the Master of the Dominicans. He is writing about the loving of friends rather than of children, but the same points apply. It may appear odd to suggest that it is in our loving, in relationships with those whom we love most, that we need to learn the lesson of death, but this appears to be the curious logic of the human heart. Perhaps it is even true to suggest that our finding this an odd juxtaposition, somehow distasteful or inappropriate, indicates the distance we have to go to winning the wisdom of dispossession.

Falling in love is wonderful, whoever one is. But to believe that

[109]

being in love must involve wrapping oneself around another person is to ignore the lesson of dispossession.

The ways we love tell us whether we have learned to let go. Whoever I am, the highest form of love I can offer to another is to let go of him, to let her be herself. We can ask ourselves Father Timothy's question: does the fact that I love this person, my child, my spouse, my friend, lead that person more fully into the mystery of freedom, or does it restrict and render dependant? And am I myself made more whole by the love I feel?

A married couple with many years' experience of the joys and heartbreaks of life together and of bringing up children told me once that 'romantic love is the enemy of marriage'. Their point was that romantic love, as it is frequently presented to us, involves the partners in a relationship becoming 'all in all' to one another. There is no space left for either partner to be themselves, nor does the relationship look outwards.

The difficult lesson, whether for the celibate or for the lay person, is that we will experience pain as we seek to allow those whom we love to be who they truly are. 'He who binds to himself a joy does the winged life destroy, but he who kisses the joy as it flies lives in eternity's sunrise', as Blake puts it.[8] No one has the right to 'bind to himself' another person, although as Blake suggests, we may often try. We can try to bind others to ourselves, curtailing their freedom, their humanity, their ability to grow – but also limiting and destroying ourselves in the same process. If we can learn to walk away, not negligently or cold-heartedly, but with a passionate commitment to the well-being of the one we love, then we may both give and receive the freedom of the children of God.

I have known something of this painful dynamic both in parting from those I have cared for as students and those I have loved as friends. Walking away, which sometimes may involve disappearing from someone's life, is a little death, and we should not pretend to ourselves that it is ever easy. But joy can follow if we step into this darkness. The pain we endure in these situations is, as Radcliffe goes on to tell us, an 'opening up' – which he likens to the opening of the sides of Christ.

Medieval iconography included many symbols used to represent Christ and one of the most memorable is the pelican. According to travellers' tales of the period, the pelican was a bird which modelled self-sacrifice: it pecked open its own breast, they claimed, and fed its young with its own blood. Thus its association with the saviour, who shed his blood to redeem us all. In this process of non-possessive love we are invited to become, like Christ, pelican figures – those who open their sides for others.

The redemptive opening of Christ's side, depicted in religious art, was the birth of the Church's sacramental system: blood and water, the Eucharist and baptism. The symbolism is beautiful, and there is truth in the ideas it expresses. It is the love that opened Christ's side that redeems, and that redemption is made effectively present in the Church's sacraments.

'Can that be Love that drinks another as a sponge drinks water?'[9] asks William Blake, in another context. It is not difficult to find within oneself the unquenchable thirst to which Blake is alluding, the seemingly endless space into which we can desperately wish to hurl anyone and anything that comes our way. We see this hunger dramatised for us in the crude good-versus-evil conflicts of action movies, whose comic-book style villains, with their endless quest for world domination, are an externalisation of the hunger we can find in ourselves. In almost mythic terms, the victories of the heroes in such tales dramatise the process of dispossession, the breaking open of our hard hearts, that must happen – not once but many times – if we are to be free to love as God loves.

What is being broken open, suffering the wound of love, as we let go is our own stony heart that is constantly afraid of the river of change. That sense of myself that grasps, that choruses 'I, Me, Mine', that wants to hold on and is terrified of the consequences of letting go. The American Buddhist writer and spiritual teacher Jack Kornfield makes the point well: 'At the root of suffering is a small heart, frightened to be here, afraid to trust the river of change, to let go . . . This small unopened heart grasps and needs and struggles to control what is unpredictable and unpossessable.'[10]

Kornfield would surely agree with the medieval author of the *Theologia Germanica*: 'It is said, it was because Adam ate the apple that he was lost, or fell. I say, it was because of his claiming something for his own, and because of his I, Mine, Me, and the like. Had he eaten seven apples, and yet never claimed anything for his own, he would not have fallen: but as soon as he called something his own, he fell, and would have fallen if he had never touched an apple.'[11]

This is the most remarkable insight, because it is only too easy to suppose that advising detachment from those we love somehow diminishes our love for them. Nothing could be less true. What we should seek to surrender are the barriers that prevent us from really loving. Someone who is able to let go is someone who is truly in love, because their open heart can touch and be touched without self seeking becoming a barrier. This is a very high ideal.

It is this desire to be free of the constraints of the 'body of fear' that leads to the most radical of the monastic vows, obedience. Letting go of my own will has to be the most dynamic way of entering into freedom. This is a route fraught with peril, because the nature of monastic obedience is desperately easy to misunderstand in a variety of ways so multi-faceted that they would need a book of their own to explore. But the central reality of obedience is the letting go of grasping.

What is alarming sometimes is how, in our struggles to let go in the areas we might consider heroic, we can witness ourselves hanging on for grim death in areas that, with a moment's thought we would realise, do not matter at all. As the Buddha memorably puts it: 'Seeing misery in views and opinions, without adopting any I found inner peace and freedom. One who is free does not hold to views or dispute opinions. For a sage there is no higher, lower or equal, no places in which the mind can stick. But those who grasp after views and opinions only wander about the world annoying people'.[12]

The final sentence would certainly have appealed to the sense of humour of the author of the *Rule for Monks*.

The Desert Fathers saw the same issue as central to their asceticism: to show a visitor the true nature of detachment, one monk brought a piece of fish, badly cooked, to his senior companion. 'Isn't it good?' he asked him. 'Yes, it is good,' was the reply. The next day, the visitor watched fish delivered again to the senior, by the same monk, but this time the food was well prepared and tasty. 'I've spoiled it,' said the cook. 'Yes,' replied the elder, 'it is spoiled.'

Great stress was placed on submission to others, the conscious dispossession not of one's own will, but rather of wilfulness. This was especially important in the small things – every monk knows that obeying the Abbot (who usually addresses matters of importance) is reasonably straightforward. It is the foibles of the third under-sacristan that can drive us all to distraction.

In the case of the Desert Fathers, it was submission to one another when food was prepared that reflected great ascetical prowess: accepting spoiled fish without a murmur, for example. St Benedict would have called it 'being content with the meanest and worst' (RB7). Monks can be very reverential of one another in the choir, but take a look at them in the refectory. One elder of my own community was a substantial figure, once described as constituting a procession even when he was walking alone. He was well known for only moving in straight lines, so it was wise not to get between him and his dinner. No hostages were taken. This may not have been good for him, but it was certainly a challenge for others.

A story that has been attached to several twentieth-century guru figures tells of how the master formed a community of disciples, calling upon them to practise fraternal charity as their central discipline. One of the community was a difficult person, argumentative and critical of everyone around him. He gave the disciples a hard time, and it was with a definite sense of relief that they eventually watched him leave the community, which he said was not a really spiritual place, in his view. To their dismay, the master went after him, and persuaded him to return. He even offered to pay the man to remain. 'Loving this man,' the master told his disciples, 'is the highest form of practice'.

When we truly let go, we can become life-giving for others. The most astonishing generosity, the greatest openness, the true centres of life and of giving are found among those who know how to let go. They are not people who feel nothing – far, far from it. But they do not wrap themselves up in one another. Because they have set one another free, the love they share is poured out to all comers, and since love is not a non-renewable resource (which is how we often treat it) their love for one another grows as a consequence.

Friends who have been generous to me over the years have a tradition of 'open house' in the family home. There are always friends and passers-by at the table come mealtimes. From other friends, parents of adult children, I have learned how to care deeply for others, while leaving them free to live their own lives. Their model of loving their children and setting them free is a miracle of love in action.

And so the paradox begins to emerge, as the light fades at the end of the day, that it is when we are sufficiently aware of ourselves to let go of ourselves, that we can sincerely and lovingly reach out to others. In the Ox Herding images the final scenes are instructive. The seeker has tracked and tamed the ox that was missing, and having achieved the quest we find that the ox and the seeker both vanish from the images. We can only surrender what is ours to give. But when all is given away, when we are able to let go, we are ready for a scene that may not have been expected. In the tenth picture, the seeker has returned to the business of the everyday: 'I go to the marketplace with my wine bottle and return home with my staff. I visit the wineshop and the market, and everyone I look upon becomes enlightened.'[13] Outwardly, the holy person looks very much like anybody else: supremely ordinary. But in her freedom, she shares the love of God with everyone she meets. Because she is not afraid to let go and to walk away, the holy person does not impede love, rather, she has become love's conduit.

The gospel canticle for the Night Office, Compline, is the Song of Simeon, the *Nunc Dimittis*:

> Now, Lord, lettest thou thy servant
> Depart in peace, according to thy word

For my eyes have seen thy salvation.

(Luke 2)

To be able to walk away, to let go, we need – like Simeon – to see the sign of salvation that God extends to us in Christ. It has been my concern in this book to share the places where I have found him present: first and foremost in the people and experiences of my own life. In a Christmas sermon, Eckhart, the medieval Dominican mystic, proposes the wonderful image of the Father giving birth to the Son eternally, but asks 'what does it avail me if this birth takes place unceasingly, but does not take place within myself?'[14]

Christ is born in each one of us, unceasingly coming forth from the Father. My body, my emotions, my ideas, my actions, all can be the cradle for that birth. It is in the landscape of my own life that I can look to find the footsteps of the saviour.

The risen Christ, according to the Gospel of St John, invited Thomas 'the doubter' to probe the Lord's wounded hands, and even to place his own hand into Christ's opened side. The body, even the body of God, carries the history of our tragedies along with our triumphs. The glorified wounds are a powerful reminder that, whatever has happened to us along the way, even the damage, will become glorious, for from the opened side will living waters flow, but it is never lost. Although we step ultimately into the darkness, nothing is lost.

Notes

All biblical quotations are from the Revised Standard Version, eds. H. G. May and B. M. Metzger (Oxford University Press, 1962).

References to the Rule of St Benedict are to the edition translated by Abbot Justin McCann, *The Rule of St Benedict* (London, Burns & Oates, 1951).

Introduction
1. Muriel Spark, *The Abbess of Crewe* (New York: New Directions, 1995), p. 11.
2. Luke Elwes, *Pilgrim*, Exhibition Catalogue (London: Art First, 1998), p. 7.
3. Douglas Adams, *Life, the Universe and Everything* (London: Pan, 1980), p. 98.

Chapter 1: The Piper at the Gates of Dawn
1. W. H. Auden, 'For the Time Being', in *Collected Poems* (London: Faber & Faber, 1976), p. 286.
2. T. S. Eliot, 'Ash Wednesday', in *Collected Poems and Plays* (London: Faber & Faber, 1969), p. 89.
3. The Ox Herding images can be found in several published sources, for example: Paul Reps, *Zen Flesh, Zen Bones* (Harmondsworth: Penguin Books, 2000).
4. Most of the sayings and stories of the Desert Fathers retold in the present book are loosely based upon Thomas Merton's collection, *The Wisdom of the Desert* (London: Burns & Oates, 1997).
5. W. H. Auden, 'In Transit', in *Collected Poems* (London: Faber & Faber, 1976), p. 413.
6. Anon., *The Cloud of Unknowing*, Chapter 13, ed. William Johnston (New York: Image Books, 1973), p. 65.
7. Ibid., p. 65.
8. A colourful example of such a procession of the principle vices is to be found in William Langland, *The Vision of Piers Plowman*, Passus V (Confession of the Seven Deadly Sins).
9. See *The Comedy of Dante Alighieri, the Florentine, Cantica 1, Hell*, translated by Dorothy L. Sayers (Harmondsworth: Penguin Books, 1949), Canto III, ix.
10. See *The Spiritual letters of Dom John Chapman*, ed. Roger Hudleston (London: Sheed & Ward, 1946), Introduction, p. 25.

11. Kenneth Grahame, *The Wind in the Willows* (Ware: Wordsworth Classics, 1992), p. 148.

12. Ibid., p. 149.

13. Ibid., p. 156.

Chapter 2: The Vision of the Way

1. C. H. Sisson, 'For Thomas à Kempis' in *Antidotes* (Manchester: Carcanet, 1991), p. 63.

2. Ibid., p. 48.

3. Wilson van Dusen, *Returning to the Source, The Way to the Experience of God*, (Moab, Utah: Real People Press, 1997).

4. William Blake, from 'Poems in Letters', in *The Poems of William Blake*, ed. W. H. Stevenson and D. V. Erdman (London: Longman, 1971), p. 475.

5. *The Comedy of Dante Alighieri, the Florentine, Cantica 1, Hell*, translated by Dorothy L. Sayers, Introduction, p. 68.

6. Sisson, p. 64.

7. Alan Ball, *American Beauty* (Basingstoke: Film Four, 2000), pp. 88–9.

8. Anon, 'In Beauty May I Walk', from the Navaho (translated by Jerome K. Rothenberg) in *The Rattle Bag*, ed. Seamus Heaney and Ted Hughes (London: Faber & Faber, 1982), p. 208.

9. H. McGregor Ross, *The Gospel of Thomas* (Longmead: Element Books, 1991), pp. 12, 53.

10. Peter Brook, *The Empty Space* (Harmondsworth: Penguin Books, 1968), p. 14.

11. Simone Weil, *The Need for Roots – Prelude to a Declaration of Duties towards Mankind* (London: Routledge & Kegan Paul, 1978), p. 41.

12. The whole of this quotation is frequently attributed to Goethe, but I have it on good authority that it actually comes from W. H. Murray, *The Scottish Himalayan Expedition*, 1951, a book of which I have been unable to locate a copy.

13. Shunryu Suzuki, *Zen Mind, Beginner's Mind* (New York: Weatherhill, 1970), p. 21.

14. Ibid., p. 22.

Chapter 3: Into the Labyrinth

1. John Donne, 'Satire 3', in John Donne, *The Complete English Poems*, ed. A. J. Smith (Harmondsworth: Penguin Books, 1971), p. 163.

2. G. M. Hopkins, 'No Worst. There Is None' in *The Poems of G. M. Hopkins*, ed. Gardner and MacKenzie (London: Oxford University Press, 1967), p. 100.

3. Guigo the Carthusian, *Meditationes Guigonis*, ed. A. Wilmart (1936) no. 149, quoted in Aelred Squire, *Asking the Fathers* (London: SPCK, 1973), p. 129.

4. S. T. Coleridge, 'The Rime of the Ancient Mariner', in *S. T. Coleridge, Poems and Prose*, ed. Kathleen Raine (Harmondsworth: Penguin Books, 1957), p. 56.

NOTES

5. Willie Russell, *Shirley Valentine* (London: Methuen, 1993), p. 30 (slightly adapted).
6. *The Comedy of Dante Alighieri, the Florentine, Cantica 1, Hell*, translated by Dorothy L. Sayers, Canto I, i-iii, p. 71.
7. Anthony Minghella, *The Talented Mr Ripley*, a screenplay based on the novel by Patricia Highsmith (London: Methuen, 2000), pp. 114–5.
8. Marie-Louise von Franz, *Archetypal Dimensions of the Psyche* (Boston: Shambala, 1999), p. 51.
9. Rust Hills, *Writing in General and the Short Story in Particular* (Boston: Mariner, 2000), p. 7.
10. The Buddha, quoted in Jack Kornfield, *After the Ecstasy, the Laundry* (New York: Bantam, 2000), p. 172.
11. Gregory the Great, *Moralia in Job,* translated and quoted by Aelred Squire, *Asking the Fathers* (London: SPCK, 1975), p. 131.
12. Roger Hudleston (ed.) *The Spiritual letters of Dom John Chapman.*
13. von Franz, Section Three, 'The Transformed Berserker: The Union of Psychic Opposites'.

Chapter 4: Tincture and Reflection
1. Jean Earle, 'The Woollen Mill', in *Visiting Light* (Bridgend: Poetry Wales Press, 1987), p. 7.
2. Henrik Ibsen, *Peer Gynt*, translated by Peter Watts (Harmondsworth: Penguin Books, 1966), p. 191.
3. Jean Earle, p. 8.
4. Sidney Piddington, 'The Special Joys of Super Slow Reading', quoted in Mark Link, *You – Prayer for Beginners and Those Who Have Forgotten How* (Niles: Argus Communications, 1976), p. 36.
5. Ibid.
6. Guigo the Carthusian, *The Ladder of Monks,* ed. and trans. E. Colledge and J. Walsh (London and Oxford: 1978), quoted in Simon Tugwell, *Ways of Imperfection*, (London: DLT, 1984), p. 94.
7. Ibid.
8. George Herbert, 'Prayer', in *A Choice of George Herbert's Verse*, ed. R. S. Thomas (London: Faber & Faber, 1967), p. 27.
9. Quoted in Tugwell, p. 94.
10. Anon., *The Cloud of Unknowing*, Chapter 7, ed. William Johnston (New York: Image Books, 1973), p. 56.
11. Bruce Chatwin, *The Songlines* (London: Picador, 1987), p. 16.
12. Luke Elwes, *Pilgrim*, p. 7.
13. Bernie Wooder, quoted by Joanna Rahim, 'Shrink Wrapped', in British Airways' *High Life* magazine, March 2000.
14. Francis Thompson, 'The Kingdom of God', in *The Poems of Francis Thompson*, ed. 'W. M.' (London: Oxford University Press, 1937), p. 350.

Chapter 5: Walking Away

1. C. Day Lewis, 'Walking Away', in *The Complete Poems* (London: Sinclair-Stevenson, 1992).

2. Antonio Machado, 'Chant XXIX, Proverbios y cantares', *Campos de Castilla*, 1917, unpublished translation in a letter to the author by Sr. Gemma Simmonds, IBVM.

3. Antonio Machado, 'Moral Proverbs and Folk Songs, no.13', in *Times Alone*, translated by Robert Bly (Hanover: Wesleyan University Press, 1983). p. 113.

4. Kabir, 'To be a slave of intensity', in *The Rag and Bone Shop of the Heart*, ed. Bly, Hillman, Meade (New York: Harper Perennial, 1992), p. 369.

5. From the *Order for the Burial of Dead Priests*, translated from the Greek by Isabel Hapgood.

6. Sogyal Rinpoche, *The Tibetan Book of Living and Dying* (London: Rider Books, 1992), p. 7.

7. Timothy Radcliffe, *Sing A New Song* (Dublin: Dominican Publications, 1999), p. 135.

8. William Blake, 'Poems from the Notebooks', no.xxxix, in *The Poems of William Blake*, ed. W. H. Stevenson and D. V. Erdman, p. 162.

9. William Blake, 'Visions of the Daughters of Albion', l.192, in *The Poems of William Blake*, ed. W. H. Stevenson and D. V. Erdman, p. 185.

10. Kornfield, p. 288.

11. Anon, *Theologia Germanica*, translated by Susanna Winkworth (London: Macmillan, 1913), p. 8.

12. The Buddha (adapted from the *Suttanipata*, translated by V. Fausboll), in Kornfield, p. 288.

13. Kakuan, '10 Bulls', no.10 *Into the World*, in Reps, *Zen Flesh, Zen Bones*, p. 147.

14. Eckhart, Sermon 21, in *Breakthrough: Meister Eckhart's Creation Spirituality in New Translation*, Matthew Fox (New York: Doubleday, 1980), p. 293.

Acknowledgements

The author is grateful for permission to reprint extracts from the following:

'For the Time Being' and 'In Transit' by W. H. Auden, from *Collected Poems* by W. H. Auden (London: Faber & Faber, 1976). Copyright © 1976 the executors of the Estate of W. H. Auden.

'For Thomas à Kempis' by C. H. Sisson, from *Antidotes* by C. H. Sisson (Manchester: Carcanet Press, 1991). Copyright © 1991 C. H. Sisson.

Writing in General and the Short Story in Particular by Rust Hills. Copyright © 1977, 1987 Rust Hills. Reproduced by permission of Houghton Mifflin Company. All rights reserved.

'The Woollen Mill' by Jean Earle, from *Visiting Light* by Jean Earle (Bridgend: Poetry Wales Press, 1987). Copyright © 1987 Jean Earle.

'Walking Away' by C. Day Lewis, from *The Complete Poems* by C. Day Lewis (London: Sinclair-Stevenson, 1992). Copyright © 1992 in this edition The Estate of C. Day Lewis.